CANADA'S
BIGGEST
SMALLEST
FASTEST
STRONGEST

by Shane Sellar

BLUE
BIKE
BOOKS

D0451150

The Publisher: Blue Bike Books Ltd.
Website: www.bluebikebooks.com

Library and Archives Canada Cataloguing in Publication

Sellar, Shane, 1978–

      Canada's biggest, smallest, fastest, strongest / Shane Sellar.

ISBN 978-1-926700-15-1

      1. Canada—Miscellanea. 2. World records—Canada. I. Title.

FC60.S45 2010   971.002   C2010-900070-6

Project Director: Nicholle Carrière
Project Editor: Nicholle Carrière
Cover Image: Photos.com
Illustrations: Djordje Todorovic, Roger Garcia, Peter Tyler, Patrick
Hénaff, Graham Johnson

We acknowledge the support of the Alberta Foundation for the Arts
for our publishing program.

We acknowledge the financial support of the Government of Canada
through the Book Publishing Industry Development Program
(BPIDP) for our publishing activities.

 Canadian Patrimoine
Heritage canadien

PC: 5

Dedication

This book is dedicated to the Cutest Canadian, Megan Sellar.

Acknowledgements

I would like to thank everyone at Blue Bike Books for once again allowing me this amazing opportunity. As far as I'm concerned you're the World's Greatest Publisher.

Contents

Introduction

Please turn off any and all electronic devices before reading this book—that includes cell phones, televisions, radio, video games and, yes, even electronic hearing aids. The journey you are about to embark on does not require synthetic noise, the power of hearing or Google, though proper lighting is essential.

In fact, the only item that you will need to bring along with you on this trek is an HB pencil—or a pen. You may also bring a crayon, chalk or charcoal, if you like. The point is, bring some type of writing utensil with you. And if you don't want to bring one along, fine, though you'll miss out on all the games and puzzles. But you don't care about fun, do you? Oh, you do. Well then, grab that charcoal and let's begin.

There is no mystery as to why Canada is nicknamed the "Great White North." It's located up north, it's covered in ice and snow most of the year, and it's the greatest country ever—though Atlantis sounds like it was a pretty cool place. However, Atlantis never had a pet name that featured the adjective "great," and you don't get a descriptor like that without being able to back it up.

Canada was born on July 1, 1867, but its record-setting ways began much earlier than the signing of the British North American Act—it began with its tectonic formation.

Geographically gifted with the world's largest trees and lowest tides, Canada is also blessed with a climate that not only freezes every weather record in its tracks but melts them like snowmen.

Even before the British, the French or the Vikings arrived, Canada's indigenous creatures were gnawing their way into the record books, thanks to the world's smallest animal and Canada's largest rodent.

As for humans, when they finally arrived, they put those critters to shame with bipedal performers like the world's tallest woman and Canada's oldest man.

What's more, Canadians turned out to be real jocks and jockettes, boasting the world's fastest man and the youngest person (a female) to swim the English Channel.

When they weren't setting records for physical feats, Canadians were setting records for structural ones, like the world's skinniest building and one of its longest national highways.

As with any great civilization, once established, the county built monuments to honour its past accomplishments, as well as its favourite foods. Massive marvels of glass, steel and hockey tape were erected across Canada's span, from the world's largest cuckoo clock, to earth's biggest Ukrainian sausage (kielbasa)—hold the sauerkraut.

Landscape, climate, beasts, Canadians, athletes, construction and marvels, in more ways than one, Canada and Canadians have broken every record there is—some while walking backwards and chewing gum.

And if you think that sounds cool, put down that piece of charcoal, grab a pencil and let's discover what else makes Canada such a superlative place.

The Funki_est Canadian

Oldest	Dumbest
Smartest	Smelliest
Youngest	Strongest
Weakest	Hottest
Happiest	Angriest
Flakiest	Funkiest
Funniest	Wickedest
Richest	Slimiest

(Superlative recommendations for chapter title—pick one or add your own)

Canadudes and Canadudettes

Being a Canadian doesn't only mean that you can stickhandle a puck while riding on the back of a Ski-Doo with a moose drinking maple syrup on your shoulders. Being a Canadian means that you can do all of that and decimate world records at the same time.

Since the inception of this great country of ours, Canadians have been filling world record book pages with such awesome feats as the world's strongest, tallest and smartest, for example. Even our governing figureheads, such as our provincial premiers and prime ministers, have tasted the sweet air of record-setting fame—and infamy, too, in some cases. But it is common Canadians who have taken it upon themselves to make this country one of the most renowned record-setting regions in the world. And not all these feats were intentional, mind you. Oh, no. Some Canadians, such as Anna Swan and the Iverson quintuplets, were setting records in height, weight and quantity from the day they were born. Others like Olga Kotelko and Marie-Louise Meilleur didn't manage to break any records until their late 90s and early 100s.

Regardless of age, though, Canadians go above and beyond when it comes to achieving world bragging rights, and even those born in other countries seem to pick up our competitive spirit when they are declared Canadian citizens. World-record recipients Sri Lankan Suresh Joachim and Englishman Alfred Revell both landed in *the record books shortly after landing in Canada. Yes, we are truly a nation of spirited competitors, scientific wonders and medical marvels all rolled into one tight little red-and-white package of record-breaking fury.*

For Whom the Dumbbells Toll....

The worst part about being the strongest man around is that all your friends want your help when they have to move. Although, in the case of **Canada's Strongest Man**, Louis Cyr could not only help you move your futon, but he could also relocate your entire house on his back.

Born in St. Cyprien de Napierville, Québec, on October 10, 1863, Cyr is still considered to be Canada's strongest man, with a number of his feats of strength still going unchallenged, even to this day.

Entering his first strongman competition at the tender age of eight, Cyr managed to lift a horse off the ground using only his bare hands. At age 17, he weighed a substantial 104 kilograms and had an appetite to match his brawn. It is rumoured that for lunch, Cyr would consume an entire pig. And while a career in eating contests was possible, Cyr's real ambition was to set weightlifting world records. For example, in 1895, Cyr managed to heave a large podium onto his back. Standing on that podium, however, were 18 fully grown, heavyset men. Combined, the total weight of the platform and its cargo was 1967 kilograms. An additional test of burliness saw Cyr lift 250 kilograms using only one finger. Simultaneously, he also hoisted 1860 kilograms onto his back and raised 124 kilograms above his head using his other hand. Combined, Cyr lifted 2234 kilograms that day, which is the equivalent of lifting a modern-day crossover sport-utility vehicle.

After he passed away on November 10, 1912, from Bright's Disease, an illness that effects kidney function, an area in Cyr's hometown of Montréal was named after him. A number of statues commemorating Cyr's buffness were erected throughout the area as well.

Le Feat

Montréal is the Largest Francophone City in North America.

Stilt-letto Heels

You know what they say about tall women—they don't get runs in their stockings, they get marathons. Born on August 6, 1846, in Mill Brook, Nova Scotia, Anna Swan is considered to be the **Tallest Canadian Female** to have ever lived. She weighed over eight kilograms at birth, and by the time she was 15 years old, Anna was well over two metres tall. Without a lot of work options for a gal of her proportions, when she turned 16, Anna did what many unusual individuals did in those days—she ran away and joined P.T. Barnum's travelling circus.

Putting her stature on show for throngs of stupefied onlookers, Anna became a main attraction of the sideshow. However, her altitude didn't only attract curiosity-seekers, it also enticed potential suitors.

While the circus toured Halifax, Anna met and fell in love with Martin Van Buren Bates. Known as the "Kentucky Giant," Bates was no stranger to heights himself.

Towering around the 2.4-metre mark, Bates was the right fit for Anna, who married him in the spring of 1871. Not ones to let their height hinder them, the colossal couple began to tour around the country billed as the **Largest Married Couple in the World**.

Anna and Martin enjoyed a happy life, though having children would always elude them. Later in life, they retreated to a quiet homestead in the country. Anna died on August 5, 1888. At the time of her death, she was 2.27 metres tall.

Bragging Rights

The rest of Canada is green with envy that Nova Scotia has the **Highest Population of Irish Canadians**.

Typo Negative

No generation in history has typed as many words as the current one. Unfortunately, thanks to the advent of texting, many of those words are completely undecipherable to anyone over the age of 40—which explains why a 16-year-old holds the title of **Canada's Fastest Texter**.

The Funkiest Canadian

Kathy Spence of Scarborough, Ontario, entered the LG Texting Championship on an impulse while shopping at the Scarborough Town Centre on June 29, 2009. Fortunately, that whim ended up making Spence $25,000 richer. Out of 20,000 other texters, Spence typed the quickest and most accurate text message: suoicodilaipxecitsiligarfilacrepus.

For the record, that's Mary Poppins' favourite saying—supercalifragilisticexpialidocious—spelled backwards.

Radio-active

Before the invention of television, people found entertainment on the radio. Not only did radio allow listeners to escape into their imagination, but the image-less device also provided unattractive people with employment (just kidding!). And though he wasn't hard on the eyes, Oscar Brand did have the **World's Longest Running Weekly Radio Program** (with the same host).

Born in Winnipeg, Manitoba, on February 7, 1920, Brand began his radio show, *Folksong Festival*, on December 9, 1945, on WNYC Radio in New York City. A renowned singer-songwriter-composer with over 300 songs and 100 albums to his name, Brand was also the recipient of a number of prestigious awards, including a Peabody and an Emmy. Brand hosted his hour-long program for 60 years, finally calling it quits on November 14, 2005.

Governing Body of Work

You don't get to become the **Longest Serving Canadian Premier** by being a "talker." You obtain that title it by being a "doer"—Gary Doer, in fact. Calling it quits on August 27, 2009, after a decade of serving as the premier of Manitoba, this twice re-elected NDP leader was also elected into the record books.

Five-Dollar Feat

Former Canadian Prime Minister Sir Wilfrid Laurier—the man on the five-dollar bill—holds the record for the **Longest Unbroken Term as Prime Minister** (15 years) and also for the **Most Consecutive Federal Elections Won** (four), making him **Canada's Greatest Statesman**.

Whoa Baby!

Get a wheelbarrow—here comes the **World's Heaviest Newborn**. Born on January 19, 1897, to **Canada's Tallest Female**, Anna Bates, this teetering toddler weighed in at 10.8 kilograms. To put that into perspective, an average newborn weighs around 3.5 kilograms. Unfortunately, the child lived for only a few hours after its birth.

Double Prescriptions

The best thing about having a twin is that you get to watch yourself grow old. And two people who would know all about that are **Canada's Oldest Twins**.

Ellen Robertson and Sarah Jeanmougin were born on May 29, 1902, to Walter and Jane Hall of Wolseley, Saskatchewan. In 2007, both Ellen and Sarah celebrated their 105th birthdays. Unfortunately, it would be their last. In December of that year, Ellen died, and Sarah followed soon after, in February 2008. Ellen once credited her record-setting age to daily exercise, clean living and spiritualism.

Medium Feat

Said to have regularly used Ouija boards, crystal balls and psychic mediums to communicate with the dead, including past prime ministers, ex-presidents, his mother and his deceased dogs, former Prime Minister William Lyon Mackenzie King was the **Most Spiritualistic Canadian Prime Minister.**

Outlive It Up

If he ever had greedy relatives waiting for him to pass away in order to collect a large inheritance, Joseph Saint-Amour certainly outlived them all. He was born in the province of Québec on February 26, 1852, and when he died on February 10, 1961, Saint-Amour was 110 years and 18 days old, making him the **Oldest Canadian Male**. What's more, he was the first person to reach the age of 110 in the 20th century.

It's a Bird, It's a Plane...It's Supercentenarian!

While it may not bestow the recipient with the ability to fly or even shuffle down the hallway faster, being a supercentenarian does mean that one has the power of longevity.

Born in Kamouraska, Québec, in 1880, Marie-Louise Meilleur holds the record for **Canada's Oldest Female**. Although she died of a blood clot in 1998 at the impressive age of 117 years, 230 days, Meilleur still retains the title over 10 years later.

As of August 2009, Meilleur was ranked number five on the list of the **World's Oldest People Ever**. She was so old that at one point, she was living in the same nursing home as her son. Conflicting causes contributed to Meilleur's elongated life, however. Although she was a staunch vegetarian who paid strict attention to her diet, she was also a devout cigarette smoker.

Bragging Rights

Take a breath of fresh air and eat a salad, British Columbia. You're the **Healthiest Province in Canada!**

Life Unexpectancy

Although Marie-Louise Meilleur holds the Canadian record for being the oldest person, Mary Josephine Ray (née Arsenault), aged 114 at this writing, is catching up to her.

Currently the **Oldest Living Person Ever Recorded in Prince Edward Island**, Ray was born on May 17, 1895.

As of 2009, Ray was considered to be the third oldest verified living person born in Canada, and she was ranked number 60 on the list of the longest-lived people ever.

Raised on PEI in the 1920s, Ray married and moved to New Hampshire. During her 80s, she spent a spell down in Florida. But on her 100th birthday, Ray's family moved her back up to New Hampshire.

A die-hard Boston Red Sox fan, Ray never misses a game. In fact, if Ray ever wanted to start her own baseball club consisting of her descendants, she wouldn't have any problems. The mother of two sons—both of whom are in their late 80s—Ray now boasts eight grandchildren, 13 great-grandchildren and five great-great-grandchildren.

Penchant for a Pension

Reaching pension age is like winning the lottery—except that you don't have enough energy to celebrate.

After paying into the Canadian Pension Plan (CPP) their whole working lives, members of Canada's Thériault family were finally old enough to collect their reward. However, no one ever thought that the event would result in the setting of a world record.

Between 1920 and 1941, Alice and Eugene Thériault had seven sons and 12 daughters. By 2007, all 19 of the Thériault siblings, ranging from 66 to 87 years in age, were collecting government pensions at the same time, becoming the **Most Siblings to Reach Pension Age**.

Brain Drain

The human body is a fascinating piece of machinery. But, like most machines, it has a tendency to have irregularities. In Victoria, British Columbia, on March 17, 1941, Theresa Alvina Schaan was born with congenital hydrocephalus, a medical condition in which fluid accumulates in the brain. Known as "water on the brain," hydrocephalus can result in an enlarged skull and, in some cases, brain impairment.

In order to relieve her condition, Schaan had to have a shunt (an alternative pathway for excess fluid to flow) inserted beneath her skull. The shunt was not only responsible for regularly draining the excess fluid from her brain, but it would also contribute to Schaan's world record.

On February 24, 2003, Schaan turned 62 years old, becoming the **World's Longest Living Hydrocephalic**.

old feat

Upon turning 80 years old on June 7, 2009, John Turner—who served the second shortest stint as PM with 79 days—became the **Oldest Living Former Canadian Prime Minister**.

Skin Deep

If you ever meet Canada's Gaulin family, you may think that they're a pigment of your imagination. As a result of a rare genetic condition known as oculocutaneous albinism, all four of the Gaulin children are albino. Sarah (September 15, 1981), Christopher (February 24, 1983), Joshua (October 25, 1987) and Brendan (July 13, 1989) all lack pigmentation in their skin, hair and eyes. The rare condition, which has left the siblings with white hair and pink eyes, has also gained the Gaulin children national recognition as the **Most Albino Siblings in the World**.

The Funkiest Canadian

Although the family was once tied for the honour with a family in the United States, in 2005, the last survivor of the competing Sesler family died, leaving the Gaulin children as the sole titleholders.

But the children aren't the only family members living with the unusual condition. Their father Mario is albino, whereas their mother Angie is simply a carrier of the gene.

Bragging Rights

Wunderbar! Saskatchewan has the **Largest Population of German Canadians**.

World's Saxiest Man

You don't usually get to be a world record holder by blowing hot air. However, in the case of Paul Brodie of Montréal, Québec, blowing is what earned him a world record.

Recognized as the **World's Most Recorded Saxophonist**, Brodie recorded almost 50 albums with his woodwind instrument and performed over 2500 concerts around the world. During his career, Brodie also did some film work, scoring the soundtrack to Warren Beatty's 1978 movie *Heaven Can Wait*. Born on April 10, 1939, Brodie founded the World Saxophone Congress in 1969. In 1994, he was made an officer of the Order of Canada. And although he passed away on November 19, 2007, Brodie's saxy tunes live on for future generations to enjoy.

Solo Can You Go?

Playing by yourself usually means that you have a body odour issue that needs to be addressed. Fortunately, that is not the case for Canadian musician Gonzales, who, on May 18, 2009, broke the record for the **World's Longest-ever Solo Concert**. Gonzales, whose real name is Jason Beck, played the piano for 27 consecutive hours, three minutes and 44 seconds in Paris, France.

No stranger to the Canadian music scene, Gonzales has collaborated in the past with such well-known Canuck acts as Feist, Buck 65 and Drake.

Touchy Feat

Considered a traitor by some and a folk hero by others for his involvement in the Red River Rebellion, the Northwest Rebellion and the formation of the Canadian Confederacy, Manitoba's Louis Riel—leader of the Métis people of the Prairies—is **Canada's Most Controversial Figure.**

Old Medal Winner

At an age when most people are having metal implanted into their hips and knees, 90-year-old Olga Kotelko is collecting metal around her neck.

Touted as the **Oldest Canadian Record Holder**, this resident of Burnaby, British Columbia, set 10 Canadian age-group records and eight world records in May 2009.

At the British Columbia Masters Championships held in Nanaimo, Olga ran the 200 metres in 1:04.16. The previous world record for her age group was 1:22.29. Furthermore, Olga went on to beat the previous discus record of 12.10 metres with an unprecedented toss of 14.58 metres. She then used her granny guns to toss the javelin 13.31 metres, beating the previous record by more than three metres. Olga also propelled the shot-put ball 4.96 metres, threw a 6.35-kilogram weight 7.72 metres and set a new Canadian record in the 100-metre dash: 21.83 seconds. But Olga's accomplishments didn't stop there. Before the 2009 Masters Championships wrapped up, Olga went on to shatter three more records in the high jump, the long jump and the triple jump.

Bragging Rights

Confucius says to celebrate, British Columbia! You have the **Highest Population of Chinese Canadians**.

A Novel Approach

Reading is the number-one pastime among people without electricity. It is also the same activity that landed thousands of school-aged children and their parents in the Canadian record books. While ABC Canada Literacy Day's attempt to dethrone the U.S. as the reigning titleholder of the **Most Children Reading with an Adult in Multiple Locations** falls short, the nearly 119,000 people who participated in the effort did manage to set a new Canadian record.

In 2009, schools from across the country participated in the "read off," which saw the Fort Nelson Community Literacy Society claim top honours, with 570 children and adults enjoying the luxuries of literature together. Following close behind, with 520 participants, was the Columbia Basin Alliance for Literacy in Revelstoke, British Columbia.

The world record of 238,620 participants, set back in 2006 by the U.S., is still undefeated.

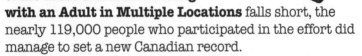

De-Feat

Following the Airbus Scandal, former Canadian Prime Minister Brian Mulroney declared that he was the **Most Investigated Prime Minister in Canadian History**.

Jack-POT!

Although criminals never prosper, they do occasionally have a turn of good luck, as in the case of Bernie Nauss of London, Ontario.

In 1997, 60-year-old Nauss was fined $25,000 for running a grow-op in his home, where he was cultivating marijuana for the purpose of trafficking.

During their raid, police seized approximately 225 pot plants from Nauss' residence. Nauss later pleaded guilty to all charges against him and paid his debt to society. However, a few months later, Nauss once again found himself surrounded by green, but this time it was the legal kind.

In March 1998, Nauss reclaimed the money he had paid in criminal fines and then some after he won $22.5 million playing the lottery.

This piece of good fortune landed Nauss the title of **Canada's Largest Single-Ticket Lottery Winner**.

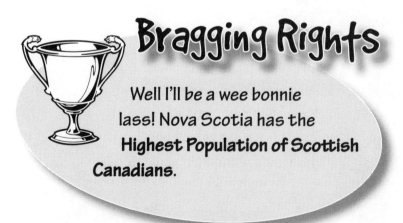

Bragging Rights

Well I'll be a wee bonnie lass! Nova Scotia has the **Highest Population of Scottish Canadians**.

Can I Quote You on That?

While some people go their whole lives without saying anything of merit, one Canadian writer has a whole "quote closet" full of sayings that have since gone on to make him the **Most Quoted Canadian in History**.

Born in Windsor, Nova Scotia, on December 17, 1796, Thomas Chandler Haliburton was a lawyer by trade but a prolific writer in his spare time. During his tenure as a writer, Haliburton forged a number of sage proverbs that are now considered to be some of the top clichés. For example, Haliburton is often credited with such popular maxims as "the early bird gets the worm"; "barking up the wrong tree"; "six of one, half a dozen of the other"; "quick as a wink"; "raining cats and dogs"; "facts are stranger than fiction"; and "jack of all trades."

But, classic adages aside, Haliburton's crowning achievement as a Canadian writer is that he is credited as being the first person to ever reference the game of hockey in a work of literature. Although he referred to the sport as "hurley on ice," nevertheless, the description of the sport that would eventually become hockey would lead to the unsubstantiated claim that Windsor, Ontario— Haliburton's hometown—is the birthplace of hockey.

Birth Wait

Mothers always like to remind their children just how long it took to give birth to them. But the next time your mom tries to use that old guilt trip on you, just tell her

about Saskatchewan's Jackie Iverson, record holder for the **World's Longest Interval Between the Birth of Quadruplets**.

On November 21, 1993, Iverson gave birth to a bouncing baby boy named Christopher. On November 29, 1993, she gave birth to a beautiful baby girl named Alexandra. On November 30, 1993, Iverson had another boy, named Matthew, and another girl, named Sarah. For the record, that was a total of nine days between the birth of her first child and her last.

I Think, I Thunk

Someone once said, "The smartest person in the room is usually the person who didn't bother coming into the room in the first place." And if you're looking for a Canadian braniac, then look no further than Northrop Frye. Born in Sherbrooke, Québec, on July 14, 1912, Frye was raised in Moncton, New Brunswick. Later in life, he rose to international acclaim as the author of *Fearful Symmetry: A Study of William Blake*, released in 1947. Frye's vast knowledge of the English poet earned him the reputation as the leading expert on all things William Blake. Furthermore, that recognition earned Frye the title of **Canada's Greatest Thinker**.

Bragging Rights

Don't skimp on the goulash, Ontario! You have the **Largest Population of Hungarian Canadians**.

The Nosebleed Section

Tall people are extremely useful: they can reach items on high shelves, they can lead basketball teams to victory, and during rainstorms, they make perfect lightning rods.

And although he didn't conduct electricity or live on a beanstalk, Édouard Beaupré was **Canada's Tallest Male**.

He was born in Willow Bunch, Saskatchewan, on January 9, 1881, and by the time he was nine years old, Beaupré was already 1.8 metres tall. At the age of 21, he measured 2.5 metres in height and weighed over 180 kilograms. Like other lofty Canucks before him, Beaupré found steady work with P.T. Barnum's travelling circus sideshow.

Unfortunately, Beaupré's time on earth was not as long as his trousers. At the age of 23, he died of tuberculosis, unable to fulfil his cherished dream of appearing at the 1904 World's Fair in St. Louis, Missouri.

It is rumoured that, even after his death, Beaupré continued to grow. A scientific anomaly, if ever there was one, Beaupré's body was subsequently embalmed and put on display in a Montréal museum. Fortunately, a few years later, his remains were removed from the museum and transported to the Université de Montréal for scientific study. It was not until July 7, 1990, that Canada's tallest male was finally returned to his hometown of Willow Bunch, where he was cremated and laid to rest.

Rockupation

Between setting up lemonade stands and selling Pokemon trading cards on eBay, youngsters don't have much in the way of career choices. An exception is Dakota Morton of Tofino, British Columbia, who at a very young age landed himself a gig as the **World's Youngest Radio DJ**.

Born in 1988, Morton was already hosting his own radio show, *Bust-A-Groove*, every Saturday morning on Tofino's CHOO-FM by the time he was 10 years old. During his weekly set, Morton would play songs and chat with listeners. Except for the lack of prank phone calls and fart jokes, Morton was every bit a professional radio DJ. *Bust-A-Groove* rode the airwaves for two years, until Morton's family moved to Port Alberni, British Columbia, where he landed a new gig at the local radio station.

Number One with an Arrow

Much like the famed thief portrayed in the film in which his song was featured, Kingston, Ontario, singer Bryan Adams stole the top spot on the music charts and never let go. Appearing in the soundtrack for the 1991 motion picture *Robin Hood: Prince of Thieves*, the song "(Everything I Do) I Do It for You," written and sung by Adams and featured on his album *Waking up the Neighbours*, holds the record for the **World's Longest Number-One Run on Any Music Singles Chart**.

Adams' ballad spent an unprecedented 39 weeks on the Canadian singles charts. Down south, the single spent seven weeks on the U.S. *Billboard* Hot 100. Adams' song even rocked the UK singles charts, holding the number-one position for 16 weeks. The song is currently ranked number 16 on *Billboard* magazine's All-Time Top 100.

Furthermore, Adams' ditty was nominated for an Academy Award for best song.

Under the Affluence

I cannot tell you where **Canada's Richest Family** lives or give you the combination to their vault, but I can tell you who they are and how they made their fortune.

Before his birth on September 1, 1923, Kenneth Thomson's father, Roy Thomson, had already amassed a huge fortune after acquiring 15 British newspaper companies. In 1976, Kenneth became head of the Thomson Corporation. In 2005, under his astute guidance, Thomson Corporation revenues were estimated to be near $9.6 billion, which included major interests in Bell Globemedia, the CTV network and the *Globe and Mail*. That same year, *Forbes* magazine ranked Kenneth Thomson as the ninth richest person in the world. In 2006, *Canadian Business* magazine declared the Thomsons Canada's richest family, with personal assets estimated to be around $22.6 billion.

Bragging Rights

Salute, Ontario! You have the **Highest Population of Italian Canadians**.

Get-Well Wishes

For most kids, the best part about receiving a birthday card is opening it to get the $10 cheque from Grandma.

However, Shane Bernier's interest in receiving birthday cards is for a less happy reason.

Diagnosed with acute lymphoblastic leukemia, the five-year-old from Lancaster, Ontario, had always dreamed of setting a new record for the **Most Birthday Cards Received**. And in the lead-up to his eighth birthday on May 30, 2007, he put that plan into action. After making a birthday wish that he could enter the *Guinness Book of Records* with the largest number of birthday cards received, Shane almost saw his wish come true.

Although he received five million birthday cards from 36 different countries, Bernier's attempt would prove unsuccessful because Guinness retired the category of Largest Number of Greeting Cards Received after a terminally ill nine-year-old was wildly successful back in 1989.

On the bright side, Shane does hold the Canadian title for the most birthday cards received. What's more, there is a rumour that Guinness World Records may create a separate category for Shane's achievement.

And the Beat Goes On...

The heart is the most vital of all human organs. Without it, how would you love or be loved? Fortunately, thanks to modern medicine, Alfred Foster Revell was not only allowed to love again, but he also set a record for being the **World's Longest Surviving Quadruple Heart Bypass Patient**.

Born in London, England, Revell immigrated to Canada later in life, taking up residence in Hamilton, Ontario. On June 17, 1978, Revell was admitted to Hamilton General Hospital, where he underwent a surgical procedure to reduce his chances of getting coronary artery disease.

Following the surgery, Revell went on to live a happy and healthy life. He died on January 16, 2009, at the age of 94—30 years and 213 days after he underwent the surgery.

Mr. World Record

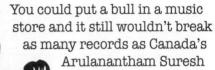

You could put a bull in a music store and it still wouldn't break as many records as Canada's Arulanantham Suresh Joachim, the titleholder of the **Most World Records**.

Originally from Sri Lanka, Suresh now calls Mississauga, Ontario, his home. Since immigrating to the Great White North, Suresh has broken 57 world records. While bragging rights are certainly a major part of the world-record-breaking business, Suresh's feats are designed to instil a far greater human emotion—empathy.

Every one of Suresh's outstanding achievements is done in a selfless attempt to bring attention to, and benefit, the underprivileged children of the world. To gain a greater appreciation for this Canadian curiosity, just check out his record-breaking collection:

☞ Farthest Distance Travelled on Escalators: 225.44 kilometres

☞ Most Star Jumps in One Minute: 62

☞ Longest Time Balancing on One Foot: 76 hours, 40 minutes

☞ Farthest Distance Run Carrying a 4.5-Kilogram Brick in an Ungloved Hand, in an Uncradled Downward Position: 126.675 kilometres

☞ Longest Radio Broadcast: 120 hours

☞ Most Bridesmaids: 79 bridesmaids

☞ Most Groomsmen: 47 groomsmen

☞ Longest Wedding Bouquet: 60.9 metres

☞ Fastest Time to Reach 100 Miles on a Treadmill: 13 hours, 42 minutes, 33 seconds

- Farthest Distance in 24 Hours on Treadmill: 257.88 kilometres
- Longest Dance Marathon by an Individual: 100 hours
- Longest Ten-Pin Bowling Marathon: 100 hours
- Longest Couples Dance Marathon with Partner: 31 hours
- Most Candles on a Cake: 150
- Most Golf Balls held in One Hand: 18 balls
- Farthest Distance to Push a Car: 19.2 kilometres
- Fastest Time to Crawl 1.6 Kilometres: 23 minutes, 45 seconds
- Fastest Time to Eat a Lemon: 30.97 seconds
- Longest Drum Marathon: 84 hours
- Longest Time Spent Watching TV: 69 hours, 48 minutes
- Longest Elvis Impersonation: 55 hours
- Longest Time Spent Watching Movies: 123 hours, 10 minutes
- Longest Time Spent Leading a Band: 42 hours, 52 minutes
- Longest Time Rocking in a Rocking Chair Continuously: 75 hours
- Longest Time Spent at an Ironing Board Continuously: 55 hours, 5 minutes

Athlete's Feat

With an uncanny knack for hockey, basketball, rugby, lacrosse, golf, baseball and tennis, Lester B. Pearson was **Canada's Most Athletic Prime Minister.**

Bodily Function

On April 1, 1993, at the age of nine years and 189 days old, Lindsay Owen of Saskatoon, Saskatchewan, became the **Youngest Person to Have His or Her Gallbladder Removed**.

An Inconvenient Toot

While the province of Alberta has all the country's gas, Manitoba is still considered **Canada's Gassiest Province**. With more flatulence than another province, the capital city of Winnipeg should consider changing its slogan from "Heart of the Continent" to "Fart of the Continent."

Bragging Rights

Throw your weight around, St. Catharines, Ontario! You're **Canada's Fattest City**.

Past His Prime Minister

In 1896, at the ripe old age of 74, Charles Tupper became the **Oldest Serving Canadian Prime Minister**. Tupper's record-setting ways, however, did not end there. Serving as Canada's sixth prime minister for only 69 days, Tupper also became **Canada's Shortest Serving Prime Minister** when he was dismissed from the position, which he held from May to July 1896, and replaced by Wilfrid Laurier.

The Funkiest Canadian

Prime Time

With over 21 years in the office, William Lyon Mackenzie King (the old, red dude on the Canadian $50 bill) is **Canada's Longest Serving Prime Minister** as well as the **Longest Serving Prime Minister in the British Commonwealth**.

Famous Feat

With a circle of friends that included The Beatles' John Lennon, a relationship with famed Canadian classical guitarist Liona Boyd, and a third-place ranking on CBC's *The Greatest Canadian*, Pierre Trudeau is **Canada's Most Popular Prime Minister**.

Over a Barrel

On October 24, 1901, Canada's Annie Edson Taylor became the **World's First Person to go Over Niagara Falls in a Wooden Barrel and Survive**.

Canadian Karats

In Tanzania, in 1939, John Williamson of Montréal, Québec, discovered the **Largest Diamond Deposit Outside South Africa**. The mine went on to yield $10 million worth of diamonds a year and is still in operation.

Last Rites

On December 11, 1962, Arthur Lucas, who was originally from the U.S., became the **Last Person to be Executed in**

Canada. Lucas, who was found guilty of the murder of an undercover officer in Toronto, was hanged alongside convicted murderer Ronald Turpin in the last act of capital punishment to be conducted on Canadian soil.

Bragging Rights

Thank God and the Pope! Catholicism is the **Most Popular Religion in Canada**.

Weightless

On January 14, 2004, with a combined weight total of 859 grams, Canada's Anne (419.5 grams) and John (439.5 grams) Morrison gained the **World's Lightest Twin Total Birth Weight** title.

Long in the Tooth

Philip Puszczalowski of Welland, Ontario, currently holds the record for **Canada's Largest Tooth Extraction**. The chiclet removed from Puszczalowski's mouth measured 2.53 cm in length.

Sore Feat

The **Most-Used Medication** in Canada is painkillers.

Games People Play

1. Who was voted "the Greatest Canadian"?
    A. Terry Fox
    B. Wayne Gretzky
    C. John A. Macdonald
    D. Tommy Douglas

2. Which Canadian city has the lowest crime rate?
    A. Winnipeg, Manitoba
    B. Saguenay, Québec
    C. Charlottetown, PEI
    D. Batman, Saskatchewan

3. What is the leading cause of accidental death in Canada?
    A. Poisoning
    B. Electrocution
    C. Motorized vehicle
    D. Suffocation

4. Who was the youngest person to serve as prime minister?
    A. Brian Mulroney
    B. Joe Clark
    C. Arthur Meighan,
    D. Brian Mulroney Jr.

5. How many kidney stones were passed by the Canadian record holder for the World's Most Kidney Stones Passed Naturally?
   A. 185
   B. 1534
   C. 5704
   D. 8678

6. Residents of which Canadian city have the longest life expectancy?
   A. Halifax, Nova Scotia
   B. Richmond, British Columbia
   C. Toronto, Ontario
   D. Never-die, New Brunswick

7. What is the most common type of childhood injury in Canada?
   A. Fracture
   B. Open wound
   C. Superficial injury
   D. Strained thumb from playing too many video games

8. In the span of one year, Guinness World Records received 1433 claims from Canadians. Of those, which of the following were actual claims?
   A. World's longest time awake without drugs
   B. World's longest time repeatedly listening to the worst song ever
   C. World's longest nipple hair
   D. All of the above

9. In which territory do people have the shortest life expectancy?
   A. Northwest Territories
   B. Nunavut
   C. Yukon

Answers on page 237.

The Funkest Canadian

Timelines

The computers at Statistics Canada have just crashed, leaving the Canadian age classification system in utter chaos. Now, as a part-time census taker, it is your job to connect the following age descriptors to their proper personal benchmark.

Get a driver's licence	Supercentenarian
Graduate from university	Centenarian
Retire	Denarian
Get married	Octogenarian
Enter the *Guinness Book of Records*	Vicenarian
Celebrate your last Christmas, maybe	Tricenarian
Have a midlife crisis	Nonagenarian
Have your birthday announced on the *Today* show	Sexagenarian
Spoil your grandkids	Quadragenarian
Move to a care home	Quinquagenarian
Be eligible for the seniors' menu	Septuagenarian

Answers on page 237.

Immigration Frustration

The computers at Immigration Canada are on the fritz, which means that they are unable to process any new Canadian citizens until the problem is fixed. Now, as a junior immigration agent, it is your job to decipher each of the place names on the list below, so that immigration officers know exactly where these new Canadians are coming from.

FSHANITAGAN_____

ICTANRACAT _____

NIAGTRAEN _____

RATAISAUL _____

LGNASAHDEB _____

COIAATR _____

AIHTPEIO_____

DGAOLUPEUE _____

EISOIANND _____

JACAIMA _____

BIMBAZWE _____

NZEVLEUAE _____

GYUAURU_____

LISWAANDZ _____

OASLMAI _____

PILHPIIPENS _____

ARNAUGCIA _____

OLSA _____

DAACAARMSG_____

AREAIMC_____

Answers on page 238.

The FUNKest Canadian

Canada's Wall of Defame

Using the featureless face provided below, please draw your interpretation of the **Weirdest-Looking Canadian**. If you need some help coming up with some truly tasteless facial features, here is a list of possible protuberances and other pustules that can be added to your mangled mug:

Black eye, no eyes, warts, missing teeth, zits, bad moustache, ratty sideburns, unibrow, open scar, fangs, pig nose, goofy glasses, buckteeth, rat tail, cauliflower ears, no eyebrows, boil, big chin, snotty nose, thin lips, rotting teeth, mullet, medical stitches...

Career Crossroads

You are tired of having so many occupations, so you're looking for a new career path. Using the clues provided below, fill in the career crossword and find yourself a new and exciting profession.

ACROSS
4. Always wired
5. Rhythmic by trade
8. Baby-kisser
9. Tip-toer
10. Suds server
12. Stuntman
13. 911 responder
14. Number cruncher
16. 3-D designer

DOWN
1. Rock star
2. Penny protector
3. Wingman or woman
6. Pipe dreamer
7. Bar examiner
8. Prone to strokes
11. Prefers pens
12. Quack
15. Rises to the occasion

Answers on page 238.

Family Find

The Canukerson family was supposed to be at the photo studio an hour ago to have their family portrait taken. They must be lost. Now, as the photographer's assistant, it is your job to go out onto Lexicon Avenue and search the busy sidewalk until you locate all the Canuckersons.

```
G A T S S D S I G Q U A D R U P L E T S G
R S N I W T D I O Y R D B S S E S E S E O
A I R T T E O G D S S B S T T R I L Y P D
N B I E C P C E R T D R T G E S S C T T M
D L P E D U E R E H G O P O P O S N E U O
S I I D G R A N D M A T Q D S N T U P P T
O N Q A L A D G C O Y H U S O T E S Q L H
N G U U E Y B A B H E E R T N R P E U E E
S T E P D A U G H T E R E H T O M T S T R
G S T E P M O T H E R I S U E V S H O S D
R N O S T Y S R I R E E D T R E A U N T N
N I S U O C N I E D C O T W E R N P R O E
O G O D F A T H E R Q C U S P L O I S C P
S T E P F A T H E R U T C H I E P S O T H
T A P H D A A P D N A R G S U S R I P D E
H D L S F H O O C T U P L E T S E W R E W
N O S D O G G R A N D D A U G H T E R T S
```

Mother	Triplets	Grandson
Father	Quadruplets	Granddaughter
Brother	Septuplets	Stepfather
Sister	Octuplets	Baby
Grandma	Cousin	Godfather
Grandpa	Nephew	Godmother
Uncle	Niece	Godson
Aunt	Stepdaughter	Tiger
Sibling	Stepmother	Rover
Twins	Stepson	

The _Mildest_ Climate

Windiest	Hottest
Coldest	Brightest
Snowiest	Rainiest
Cloudiest	Foggiest
Iciest	Chilliest
Mildest	Driest
Wettest	Moistest
Deadliest	Dewiest
Muggiest	Slushiest

(Superlative recommendations for chapter title—pick one or add your own)

Ice and Breezy

If it were not for our erratic climate, Canadians would have nothing to complain or talk about. The whole country is pretty much obsessed with the weather. For example, is there another country in the world that has a television station solely dedicated to reporting on weather? (Well, okay, there might be a few others.) Are there any other countries as fixated on half-hourly weather updates or committed to annual agricultural almanacs as much as Canucks are? Not likely. Canadians are fanatical when it comes to weather, and why not? When you live in a country that has seven seasons—spring, summer, fall and winter, plus avalanche, tornado and hurricane seasons—you are no doubt going to be glued to the daily forecast.

But it's not all sleet, snow, fog, sun, rain and wind in the Great White North. There is nary a weather condition that Canadians have not endured at some point in history. If you are unconvinced of this turbulent relationship between Canadians and our climate, just open a Canadian clothes closet. From New Brunswick to British Columbia, you will find a sunhat sitting next to a balaclava; a pair of flip-flops adjacent to a set of rubber boots. While most people would suggest that Canadians have an unhealthy relationship with the weather, the truth is, we simply desire to tame and understand it.

As potentially disastrous natural phenomena, earthquakes and tsunamis are also included here in the weather section.

Cold Turkey

The only thing that Albertans were giving thanks for over the 2009 Thanksgiving long weekend was for indoor heating. On the **Coldest Thanksgiving Weekend in Alberta**, the temperature in Calgary on October 12 (holiday Monday) was −16°C. The record low broke the previous record of −13°C set back in 1928. The same day, the mercury in Banff National Park dropped to a dismal −22°C. The abnormally frosty October temperatures were the result of a blast of cold Arctic air from the Northwest Territories. To show just how out of the ordinary these temperatures were, three weeks earlier, the temperature in Calgary was 33°C—**Canada's Hottest Day of 2009**.

Bragging Rights

Windsor, Ontario, is the
Most Humid City in Canada.

Long-Range Forecaster

Predicting the weather is a lot like foretelling the lottery. However, if you wrongly predict the jackpot numbers, people don't tend to throw snowballs and umbrellas at your head. And someone who probably has a number of war wounds to speak of is Dave Devall of Toronto, Ontario, the record holder for the **World's Longest Career as a Weather Forecaster**.

Blowing onto the meteorology scene in the early 1960s, Devall landed himself a forecasting gig on Toronto's CFTO-TV. After weathering the snowstorms and dealing with an array of atmospheric pressures for 48 years, two months and 27 days, Devall bid bon voyage to his prognosticating profession. His departure from the green screen was met with a heavy downpour of sentiment from colleagues and morning commuters. In his honour, the Channel Nine Court thoroughfare in downtown Toronto was renamed Dave Devall Way. But that's not the only silver lining in Devall's cumulus cloud. On April 3, 2009, Devall's enduring employment as a weatherperson landed him in the *Guinness Book of Records*, where his record continues to stand up to the elements.

Light feat

In 1970, British Columbia received 2426 hours of sunlight. It was the **Longest Sunny Stretch** in the province's history.

Blowing in Debris

Weather can be a two-sided coin: on one side, it can bring warmth and sunshine; on the other side, it can bring death and destruction. The following is a weather record of the latter kind.

On June 30, 1912, a balmy summer day in Regina, Saskatchewan, quickly deteriorated into a hellish nightmare when **Canada's Deadliest Tornado** cut a swath through the city, killing 28 people and injuring hundreds of others.

Widely known as the Regina Cyclone, the devastating windstorm—which consisted of a pair of green-tinged funnel clouds—

gathered on the south side of the city around 4:45 PM before it twisted its way through the bustling downtown business district. Ravaging nearly 500 office buildings and leaving 2500 people homeless, the F4-ranked tornado caused over $1.2 million in damage. Surprisingly, though, the wicked weather was not the only "monster" in town that day.

At the time that the cyclone hit Regina, British actor William Henry Pratt was in town, starring in a stage play. Appalled by the destruction that he witnessed, Pratt, who would later go on to change his name to Boris Karloff and star as Frankenstein's monster in the 1931 film version of Mary Shelley's horror classic, volunteered as a rescue worker in the wake of the worst windstorm to ever hit the prairies. Years later, the famed actor would recount his time as a Regina Cyclone rescue worker on Canada's long-running game show, *Front Page Challenge*.

Bragging Rights

Terrible Twister

In the movies, tornadoes are known for transporting unsuspecting Kansas farm girls to magical worlds. In reality, all these terrible twisters really do is destroy lives and property.

On what became known as Black Friday—July 31, 1987—the city of Edmonton was struck by the **Most Devastating Tornado in Alberta**.

Considered to be the second-deadliest tornado in Canada, after the Regina Cyclone, the Black Friday Tornado remained on the ground for an hour, cutting a 40-kilometre-long swath and leaving 27 people dead and more than 200 others injured. In total, 400 people were left homeless and an estimated $250 million in damage was caused by the tornado's winds, which were in excess of 333 kilometres per hour.

The tornado was first sighted just before 3:00 PM on the outskirts of Edmonton, near the city of Leduc. By 3:04 PM, the first tornado warning had been issued. One half-hour later, the twister was confirmed as an F4 tornado, though to this day, many people claim that it actually reached F5 classification—the worst ranking on the Fujita scale.

While the incident has gone down in infamy, the safety measures put in place following its occurrence have gone on to save lives.

In the wake of the Black Friday Tornado, the Emergency Public Warning System was put into practice throughout Canada. The warning system updates the public about hazardous weather conditions before they occur, via radio or television. A few years later, police forces across Canada began to implement the same warning system to notify the public of missing children. Today, that police warning is now recognized around the world as an Amber Alert.

Bragging Rights

Yellowknife, Northwest Territories, has the **Sunniest Summers in Canada**.

Better Never Than Late

It appears as though tornados can sometimes be like public transit—late. Ripping its way through Mont-Saint-Hilaire, Québec, on November 16, 1989, that tornado is considered to be **Québec's Latest in the Year Tornado**.

Typically, tornado season in Québec runs from May through September, with June and July being prime twister times. However, the Mont-Saint-Hilaire Tornado appeared to have misplaced its calendar, arriving two months after the deadline. Recorded as an F2 tornado, meaning its wind speed was between 181 and 253 kilometres per hour, this Johnny-come-lately funnel cloud caused an estimated $2 million in damage.

Water World

Water has the ability to clean your hands and face, but it also has the power to wash away homes, as over 4000 families in the Greater Toronto area

discovered in the wake of Hurricane Hazel.

Causing what is reputed to be **Canada's Most Severe Flood**, Hurricane Hazel dumped more than 180 millimetres of rain onto Toronto on October 14 and 15, 1954. During that 24-hour period, roads were washed away, $135 million in damage was incurred, and over 80 people died. Nearly 800 Canadian military officers were deployed to the troubled area to help with the rescue effort. Because of the sizeable death toll associated with the category 4 hurricane, the name Hazel was retired from usage in the annual hurricane-naming schedule.

Bragging Rights

Medicine Hat, Alberta, has the **Driest Weather in Canada**.

Dent from Above

Forget the sunbonnet. When visiting Cedoux, Saskatche-wan, in summer, make sure you bring a hard hat. During a hailstorm in August 1973, **Canada's Largest Hailstone** fell from the sky. Weighing 290 grams and with a diameter of 10 centimetres, the icy sphere was the size of a grapefruit.

Soaking Feat

On October 6, 1967, Ucluelet Brynnor Mines, British Columbia, received 489.2 millimetres of rain in a 24-hour period. This was the **Highest One-day Rainfall in Canadian History**. This wet event is ranked number nine on the list of the world's greatest rainfalls.

Shake and Quake

Although earthquakes on the prairies are rare, they do occur. Over 100 years ago, **Saskatchewan's Strongest Earthquake** really shook things up.

At approximately 10:00 PM on May 15, 1909, the largest known earthquake in the Northern Plains region struck. While the 5.5-magnitude tremor was considered to be moderate, it did manage to rattle a few nerves. With an epicentre located in southern Saskatchewan, near the U.S. border, the quake was felt in the eastern portion of Montana and the western half of North Dakota. Tremors even rumbled their way to the neighbouring provinces of Alberta and Manitoba. Fortunately, thanks to the lack of development in southern Saskatche-wan at the time, the 1909 earthquake did not cause much damage, except for knocking over a few cows.

Bragging Rights

Yellowknife, North-
west Territories, has the
Coldest Winters in Canada.

Ice Storm of the Century

An ice storm is helpful when you're looking for a way to cool down your soda, but when the ice storm lasts for six straight days, ice cubes are the last thing on your mind.

Canada's Worst Ice Storm hit on January 4, 1998. A lethal combination of ice, snow and rain, the storm dropped 120 millimetres of freezing rain (double the amount of the 1961 Montréal ice storm) on parts of Québec, Ontario and Nova Scotia. The ice buildup downed power lines, leaving four million people without electricity for days, and some of them for weeks. The ice also damaged trees, rendered city streets impassable and closed down bridges and tunnels throughout the Montréal area because of concerns over the weight of the chunks of ice that were forming on the structures.

On January 7, after three days of bone-chilling bombardment, Ontario and Québec called in the Canadian Forces, which arrived the next day. Over 15,000 troops were deployed to the iced-in areas in what is considered to be the **Largest Deployment of Troops Ever to Serve on Canadian Soil in Response to a Natural Disaster**. The effort was also the **Largest Operational Deployment of Canadian Military Personnel Since the Korean War**. After the storm subsided on January 10, the Great Ice Storm of 1998 left between $5 and $7 billion in damage. The ice storm also claimed the lives of 28 Canadians and injured hundreds of others.

Bragging Rights

Snow Way

Snow may look innocent, but it's one of the deadliest forms of weather if the conditions are just right, as they were on March 5, 1910, when **Canada's Deadliest Avalanche hit**.

While 60 Canadian Pacific Railway crewmembers worked to clear piles of snow that had been left by a recent landslide in a section of Roger's Pass in British Columbia, they were blindsided by a second landslide. Only two of the 60 crewmembers survived to tell the horrible tale of what transpired on that mountainside. Many of those who lost their lives that day were Japanese immigrants who were working for the CPR at the time. To prevent any further loss of life, the eight-kilometre-long Connaught Tunnel was constructed underneath Roger's Pass. When it opened in 1916, the tunnel was considered to be the **Longest Railway Tunnel in North America**.

Epicentre of Attention

If you thought that you tipped the scales after a night at the all-you-can-eat buffet, that's nothing compared to **Canada's Largest Earthquake**. Tipping the Richter scale with a magnitude of 8.1, Canada's biggest quake hit Haida Gwaii (Queen Charlotte Islands) off the coast of British Columbia on August 22, 1949. The sparsely populated islands are located on a major ocean floor fault line that extends from Vancouver Island to the Gulf of Alaska, and although the quake caused a number of landslides, there were no fatalities. However, on the mainland, 200 kilometres away, store windows shattered and buildings swayed as a result of the record-setting tremor. Residual waves were felt as far away as Alberta, the Yukon and Alaska.

Unnatural Disaster

Canada's east coast is no stranger to strange weather, but who would have ever imagined a day when the Rock would be rocked so hard? On November 18, 1929, a 7.2-magnitude earthquake occurred 400 kilometres off the southern coast of Newfoundland and Labrador in the Atlantic Ocean. The massive quake generated a tsunami (giant wave) that would eventually lead to the **Largest Death Toll for a Canadian Earthquake**.

The South Shore Disaster, as it would become known, saw a set of three massive tsunami waves roll across the

Grand Banks to Newfoundland and Labrador. The waves, which travelled at 105 kilometres per hour, struck the mainland nearly three hours after the earthquake occurred.

When the towering waves—up to 13 metres high in some places—reached shore, their immense power snapped telegraph cables and drowned 27 people. The waves were so potent that they were recorded as far away as Portugal.

Bragging Rights

You're out of sight, St. John's, Newfoundland and Labrador—literally. With 121 fog-filled days per year, St. John's is **Canada's Foggiest City**.

The Fiendish Fog

Who would have ever thought that fog—a thick cloud of water droplets—could ever be the cause of **Canada's Worst Marine Disaster**? But it was. On May 29, 1914, the Royal Mail Ship *Empress of Ireland* fell victim to poor visibility brought on by a fiendish fog and collided with a Norwegian coal freighter on the St. Lawrence River, 16 kilometres east of Pointe-au-Père, Québec. En route from Québec City to Liverpool, England, the majestic 174.1-metre-long ocean liner sank in less than 14 minutes, dragging over 1000 souls to the bottom of the river.

A Costly Catastrophe

Weather is an insurance company's arch nemesis. And that rivalry has never been more heated as it was during

Canada's Most Expensive Natural Disaster. On September 7, 1991, a hailstorm hit Calgary, Alberta. The unexpected storm may have only pelted pellets of frozen water over the Prairie province for just a few minutes, but it managed to make a lasting impression— especially on cars, homes and office buildings. In total, the hailstorm caused $400 million in damage.

Bragging Rights

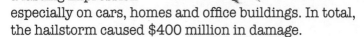

Move over London, England, here comes Collins Bay, Saskatchewan. Wandering through a total of 60 straight days of fog back in 1980, Collins Bay holds the record for the **Most Fog Days in Saskatchewan.**

Slow the Flow

Up until the Great Ice Storm of 1998, the flooding of the Red River near Winnipeg, Manitoba, was **Canada's Single Largest Military Deployment Since the Korean War.** In the spring of 1997, after the melting of the snow left by a late-winter blizzard, the Red River, which flows northward into Canada's Lake Winnipeg from Fargo, North Dakota, was inundated with spring runoff. With hundreds of homes threatened by the rising waters of the Red, 8500 members of the Canadian Forces were deployed to the region. During their time there, our military personnel helped citizens and homeowners fill sandbags, which were used to fortify the barriers designed to keep the raging waters of the Red River at bay. The threat eventually subsided, but a similar flood occurred almost 10 years later in 2009, with the Red River cresting at 6.9 metres.

Dark Feat

If you are a vampire, you may want to make Prince Rupert, British Columbia, your next vacation destination. With a record 6123 hours without so much as a ray of sunshine, Prince Rupert is **Canada's Least Sunny City**.

Gale Farts Winds

If you ever pass gas in Cape Hopes Advance, Québec, please do so downwind. On November 8, 1931, for the duration of one hour, the wind was recorded at a speed of 201.1 kilometres per hour—**Canada's Highest Sustained Wind Speed**.

Bragging Rights

Winnipeg, Manitoba, has the **Sunniest Winters in Canada**.

The _____est Climate

Wicked Weather Winner

Although every Canadian province and territory experiences a certain amount of wicked weather every year, no province or territory holds as many weather records as British Columbia.

Titleholder of the **Most Canadian Weather Records**, British Columbia has a collection of crowning climate achievements, including, **Rainiest Place in Canada**—Ocean Falls, with an annual rainfall of 440 millimetres; **Least Snowfall in Canada**—Victoria, with an annual snowfall of 44 centimetres; **Wettest Weather in Canada**—Prince Rupert, with an annual rainfall of 3111 millimetres; and **Warmest Summers in Canada**—Kamloops, with summer highs sometimes reaching 40°C.

Bragging Rights

You're so bright, Estevan, Saskatchewan. With 2510 hours sunshine annually, you are the **Sunniest Place in Canada**.

First-Place Loser

Being first usually entails accolades and awards; however, having the **First F5 Tornado in Canada** isn't much to celebrate.

On June 22, 2007, Elie, Manitoba, was hit by tornado with winds in excess of 417 kilometres per hour. Fortunately, no one was injured in the windstorm. However, it did manage to overturn vehicles, tear down power lines and force a transport truck off the Trans-Canada Highway into a ditch. In total, the tornado caused $4 million in damage.

Whiteout Side

With 75 straight days of blistering blizzards, the territory of Nunavut holds the Canadian record for the **Most Days of Blowing Snow**.

A Parched Place

A small Inuit hamlet on the northern part of Baffin Island, the community of Arctic Bay, Nunavut, is the **Driest Place in Canada**.

In 1949, the area received a mere 12.7 millimetres of precipitation for the whole year. This lack of moisture may explain Arctic Bay's failing umbrella industry.

Wetfeat

On October 6, 1967, Ucluelet, on Vancouver Island, received 1870 millimetres of rain. It was **Canada's Rainiest Day**.

Heat Wave

While it's physically impossible to spend your summer vacation on the sun, here's a list of Canadian cities that come pretty close, with the **Most Hot Days** (a daily high temperature of 30°C or above) on average per year:

Kamloops, British Columbia	29 days
Penticton, British Columbia	26 days
Kelowna, British Columbia	25 days
Medicine Hat, Alberta	23 days
Windsor, Ontario	21 days
Moose Jaw, Saskatchewan	20 days
Estevan, Saskatchewan	19 days
Vernon, British Columbia	17 days
Portage la Prairie, Manitoba	16 days
Lethbridge, Alberta	16 days

Bragging Rights

With an average wind speed of 24 kilometres per hour, St. John's, Newfoundland and Labrador, blows away the competition as **Canada's Windiest City.**

Gust or Bust

Kite enthusiasts and pinwheel fanatics take heed. The following are the **Windiest Canadian Cities**:

St. John's, Newfoundland and Labrador	23.33 km/h
Gander, Newfoundland and Labrador	20.53 km/h
Summerside, PEI	20.03 km/h
Swift Current, Saskatchewan	19.74 km/h
Regina, Saskatchewan	18.63 km/h
Sydney, Nova Scotia	18.58 km/h
Estevan, Saskatchewan	18.44 km/h
Lethbridge, Alberta	18.20 km/h
Moose Jaw, Saskatchewan	17.72 km/h
Charlottetown, PEI	17.44 km/h

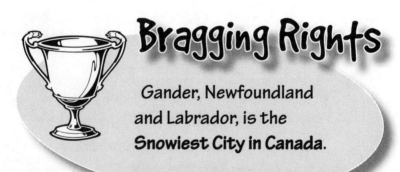

Bragging Rights

Gander, Newfoundland and Labrador, is the **Snowiest City in Canada.**

Canada's Top One-Day Snowfalls

Although Tahtsa Lake, BC, holds the record for the **Most Snowfall (145 centimetres) in a 24-Hour Period**, there are other times and places when the snowfall in a 24-hour period has exceeded 100 centimetres:

Pleasant Camp, British Columbia	127 cm on December 4, 1985
Cap Madeleine, Québec	122 cm on March 20, 1885
Lakelse Lake, British Columbia	118 cm on January 17, 1974
Stewart, British Columbia	106 cm on January 16, 1976
Kemano, British Columbia	104 cm on January 11, 1968
Nain, Newfoundland and Labrador	103 cm on January 6, 1988

Cold Feat

In the winter of 1955–56, Pelly, Saskatchewan, received 386 centimetres of snow. It was the **Greatest Snowfall in Saskatchewan's History**.

Quizzard Warning

1. Which of the following is the highest city in Canada?
   A. Rossland, British Columbia
   B. Airdrie, Alberta
   C. Kimberly, British Columbia
   D. Skyscraper, British Columbia

2. Which of the following is the highest town in Canada?
   A. Lake Louise, Alberta
   B. Banff, Alberta
   C. Elkford, British Columbia
   D. Rossland, British Columbia

3. What is the lowest temperature ever recorded in Canada?
   A. −45˚C
   B. −57˚C
   C. −63˚C
   D. The thermometer became a popsicle.

4. What is the highest temperature ever recorded in Canada?
   A. 35˚C
   B. 45˚C
   C. 52˚C
   D. I wish the thermometer was a popsicle.

The _____ est Climate

5. What is the hottest city in Canada?
    A.   Kamloops, British Columbia
    B.   Fredericton, New Brunswick
    C.   Melfort, Saskatchewan
    D.   Windsor, Ontario

6. What is the driest province in Canada?
    A.   British Columbia
    B.   Alberta
    C.   Saskatchewan
    D.   Nunavut

7. What is the snowiest city in Canada?
    A.   Winnipeg, Manitoba
    B.   Gander, Newfoundland and Labrador
    C.   Whitehorse, Yukon
    D.   Snowmonton, Alberta

8. How long did Saskatchewan's longest wet period last?
    A.   100 days
    B.   165 days
    C.   180 days
    D.   Somebody call Noah

9. What was the greatest one-day snowfall in Canada?
    A.   118 cm
    B.   135 cm
    C.   145 cm
    D.   210 cm

10. Which of the following is the windiest city in Saskatchewan?
    A.   Swift Current
    B.   Regina
    C.   Saskatoon
    D.   Blow-Me-Down

Answers on page 238.

Inclement Weather Connector

The computers at the weather station have crashed, and all the old data files have been rearranged. Now, as a meteorologist, it is your job to sort through the natural disasters and link them up to their respective places of occurrence.

Regina	Tsunami
Winnipeg	Avalanche
Québec	Nor'easter
Newfoundland	Ice storm
Edmonton	Thunderstorm
British Columbia	Tornado
Maritimes	Flooding
Northwest Territories	Cyclone
Ontario	Wind chill

Answers on page 238.

The _____est Climate

Torrential Textual Twisters

A number of weather-related words have been caught in the verbal vortex of a destructive text twister. Now, as Canada's top storm chaser, it is your job to save the terms from the wicked whirling winds of the funnel cloud and twist them back to normal.

ALNAMAC _____

OOSTMELEGRIOT _____

IIYBLVTSII _____

ORHETMMREET _____

REZEEB _____

AONDENCSNITO _____

DRHTOUG _____

ETVAINRAOOP _____

GLNTIHGNI _____

IETPIANIOCPRT _____

MUTHYDII _____

AMSERJTTE _____

ONRETMMEAE _____

DLCOU _____

MNVETOENRIN _____

ITDNGFRI _____

LUUMCUS _____

ELRAC _____

CLEPRPI _____

AYDRISVO _____

Answers on page 239.

Crossword Play

You want to enter your solar-powered car into a race across Canada. But before you can qualify for the contest, you must finish the following weather-related crossword.

ACROSS

2. Rainstorm conclusion
5. Snowstorm occurrence
8. Winter storm or summer treat
9. A student's favourite season
11. Follows an underwater eruption
13. They bring May flowers (plural)
15. A beach essential
16. Portable canopy

DOWN

1. Arch-enemy of thaw
3. A kite's best friend
4. What April showers bring (plural)
6. Nature's eraser
7. Dracula's bedtime
10. Newfoundland pea soup
12. A winter instrument
14. Forecasting tool

Answers on page 239.

The _____est Climate

Word Whiteout

While on their way to the annual meteorology convention in Brandon, Manitoba, the following weather terms got lost in the worst blizzard of the year. Now, as a member of the snow patrol, it is your job to head out into that blizzard and locate the missing words.

```
O A E Q A E H G A D F T S P H E A W O N S
V N M U T U A L T R R H L U E S E L A E E
E O N E Z R Z I E A O I E Z L N R O P A V
R S O Z O N E A R I S E Z L I O E A U R E
C U R T H U N D E R T R T Z Z S L E E T A
A N E S S E O H T M A T E C L A O S A R T
S S T A P A C A E R I I S A W E D E G E E
T E A L I N E I M O L D O S E S O T N A M
E T L I A S D U O L C E E T R U A M I W P
S C I L T A Y S R G L A C I E R L O R O E
T I A E H Z G L A G I S E E T M E N P N R
E V H Y U E G E B Y M T A Y E P S A S T A
A L E G N N A E E T A O S S G O M S Y D T
M H R G I U D W A H T N L U N G E E S E U
A E K A U Q H T R A E R U N I T U A E R R
N B R E A K E S O E R E S E S A E M A E E
L A O S M M R O T S I T H R R E T N I W A
```

Autumn	Earthquake	Rain	Sunset
Air	Frost	Seasons	Thunder
Avalanche	Glacier	Smog	Tide
Barometer	Haze	Slush	Winter
Clouds	Hail	Sleet	Temperature
Climate	Muggy	Snow	Vapor
Drizzle	Overcast	Storm	
Dew	Ozone	Spring	

The <u>Rar</u>est Beasts

Loudest	Smelliest
Hairiest	Slowest
Stupidest	Scariest
Tastiest	Deadliest
Stickiest	Rarest
Cutest	Cuddliest
Wildest	Gentlest
Largest	Smallest
Tamest	Lamest

(Superlative recommendations for chapter title—pick one or add your own)

Cananimal Instincts

Not your typical indigenous wildlife, Canadian animals, or Cananimals, are different beasts altogether. Where else in the world can you see a beaver, a moose and a black bear dressed up like Mounties for the amusement of tourists? And how about our fair-weather fowl friends, Canada geese? They visit us for the summer, then ditch us and head down south at the first sign of a falling leaf. Lame. The same goes for monarch butterflies and any other migrating animal that hangs out up north for the hot months but doesn't bother to stick out the winter like a real Cananimal.

Luckily, during the dreary, dark months, the country has a plethora of paw pals such as polar bears and arctic foxes to keep our critter quota up. What's more, this animal-friendly nation not only boasts the world's largest and smallest animals, but also the dumbest and the second fastest animals in the world. For all intents and purposes, Canada is pretty much one giant animal sanctuary. From near-extinct attractions like the bison to completely extinct entities like the dinosaurs, the Great White North is a coast-to-coast corral containing the best beasts the continent (and the world) has to offer. For that reason, tourists from around the globe travel to our shores, mountains and plains to catch a glimpse of our wildlife. Be it a polar bear up north, a blue whale on the coast or an intrusive squirrel in Banff, Cananimals are tourist attractions in themselves. So get down on all fours and wag your tail—it's time to take a walk on the wild side.

Rabid Fan Base

Not only is its fan base a fervent group, there's a pretty good chance that the **World's Most Famous Squirrel** is likely rabid itself. In May 2009, while a couple from Minnesota were taking a picture of themselves to commemorate their visit to Banff, Alberta, their portrait was interrupted by a curious Columbian ground squirrel, which stuck its furry face into the frame—and into infamy. It was dubbed the "Crasher Squirrel," and the funny photo featuring the fuzzy critter quickly made the rounds to every news station in the world. The intrusive nutter even became an Internet sensation, spawning numerous parodies of the Crasher Squirrel intruding on historical photos. Following the media and Internet coverage, curiosity seekers from around the world flocked to the national park to catch a glimpse of the superstar squirrel. Banff capitalized on the sudden popularity of its resident rascal by installing a massive billboard along Highway 1 and featuring the Crasher Squirrel on the town's website.

Sucks to Be Here

You'll need wooden stakes the size of safety pins if you hope to exterminate the "Prairie vampires." Or else you could just swat them away with your hand or a rolled up newspaper. Considered by entomologists (bug scientists) to be the **Worst Place in the World for Mosquitoes**, Churchill, Manitoba, is home to an estimated 12.5 million bloodsuckers per hectare of land.

Hooray for the giant water bug! Able to reach lengths of around 6.5 centimetres, it is considered to be **Canada's Largest Non-Moth Insect**.

Where Eagles Dare

The community of Brackendale is every patriotic American's dream. Unfortunately, for nationalistic Yanks, the **World's Largest Bald Eagle Hangout** is not located in the U.S.—it's in Canada. Immediately north of Squamish, British Columbia, on the Sea-to-Sky Highway, this avian hotspot attracts nearly 4000 bald eagles in some years. Arriving in the month of November and staying until February, the white-headed raptors are attracted by the high concentration of salmon in the area, especially at the Tenderfoot Creek Fish Hatchery.

Dam Rodents

Rodents are gnawing creatures that must constantly chew in order to keep their continuously growing incisors in check. As such, anyone with a wooden leg should avoid them at all costs. Considered to be **Canada's Largest Rodent**, the beaver was hunted by early explorers for its satiny pelt. The pelts were sent to Europe and used to make beaver-pelt hats, which were very much in vogue throughout the 1600s and 1700s.

The beaver's popularity across the pond nearly led to its extinction in Canada. Fortunately, the bucktoothed beast did not end up just another fashion victim. Instead, it went on to become the national symbol of Canada. Serving as the "tails" portion of the Canadian nickel since 1937, the Canadian beaver was also prominently featured on what is considered to be Canada's first-ever postage stamp, the Three-penny Beaver. Not bad for a distant cousin of the rat.

Crow's Feat

Last Mountain Lake, Saskatchewan, your National Wildlife Area is home to the **Oldest Bird Sanctuary in North America**. Established in 1887, birds of a feather love to get together here.

Petite Beak

If birds evolved from dinosaurs, then **Canada's Smallest Bird** must have come from a Tinysaurus. Just eight centimetres in length, the calliope hummingbird has a shorter tail and beak than other species of hummingbird. Found in the southern Interior of British Columbia and in the Rockies, the calliope has a reputation that exceeds its wingspan. Not only is it the smallest bird in Canada, it is also the smallest breeding bird found anywhere in North America. That is, if you can find it.

Bear Feat

Haida Gwaii (Queen Charlotte Islands) off the coast of British Columbia is home to the **World's Largest Black Bears**. *Ursus americanus carlottae* is a subspecies of black bear that is native to these islands and can grow in excess of two metres in length.

Old Grrrl

Q: How do you know when a polar bear is getting old?

A: It moves to Florida, dyes its hair blue and starts calling everybody "Sonny."

Although Debby was considered the **World's Oldest Polar Bear**, she opted to stay up north and spend her golden years in Winnipeg, Manitoba. Born in Russia in 1966, Debby immigrated to Winnipeg's Assiniboine Zoo in 1967.

The mother of six cubs, Debby defied animal age limits by far exceeding the average bear's lifespan of 20 years. When she turned 41 in 2007, the *Guinness Book of Records* recognized Debby's accomplishment. Unfortunately, after Debby celebrated her 42 birthday, her health began to wane, and on November 18, 2008, she was put to sleep. Debby's passing did not go unnoticed, however. Following the announcement, the zoo received hundreds of tributes and condolences from people and polar bears around the world.

Bear Feat

Kicking Horse Ski Resort in Golden, British Columbia, is the hibernation destination. Featuring a nine-hectare enclosed habitat, the resort boasts the **World's Biggest Grizzly Bear Refuge**.

Sleight of Paw

While the best trick that a dog could ever perform would be to pick up its own poop, being able to play the piano is pretty impressive. Chanda-Leah, a toy poodle from Toronto, Ontario, holds the world record for the **Most Tricks Performed by a Dog**. In addition to tickling the ivories, Chanda-Leah, who is often referred to as the **World's Smartest Dog**, can also perform various other types of stupid pet tricks, including riding a skateboard, solving math problems, painting a picture and playing the drums.

No stranger to the limelight, Chanda-Leah has been a regular feature on local and national news programs. She even appeared on *The Tonight Show* and *The Late Show*. But, more importantly, Chanda-Leah brought joy to those who needed it most by performing at nursing homes, elementary schools and local fundraising events. Sadly, in 2006, at the age of 12, Chanda-Leah played dead for the last time. Although there will never be another like her, a poodle named Sparkle-Dust is following in her paw prints, with nearly 300 tricks up her collar.

Horsepower

Nothing beats a scenic Sunday excursion through the countryside in a horse and carriage. But wait! What if the carriage isn't a carriage at all but a two-wheeled cart called a sulky that is being pulled by a sinewy standardbred pacer horse? What's more, how about instead of Sunday afternoon, it's Saturday afternoon, June 27, 2007. And, instead of galloping through the countryside, you're at Georgian Downs in Barrie, Ontario, setting the world record for the **Fastest Free-Legged Pacer**. Running the five-eighths-mile oval in one minute, 50 seconds, the five-year-old, Charlottetown, Prince Edward Island–trained, harness-racing sensation Astronomical and his rider, Randy Waples, broke the previous world record of 1:50.1, set in June 2002.

Bragging Rights

Bow down to the cecropia moth (giant silk moth), for it is **Canada's Largest Insect**. Found mostly on maple trees throughout the Maritimes, these intense insects start their lives as colossal caterpillars before metamorphosing into monstrous moths with wingspans of 13 centimetres.

A Long Day's Journey into Flight

Insects can fly anywhere they want, as fast as they want, because they don't have to pack any underwear for their trip. However, if monarch butterflies did have to pack underwear for their annual migration, they wouldn't be packing "briefs." Record holders for the **Longest and Largest Insect Migration in North America**, the orange-and-black insects live up to their Australian moniker of "wanderer." At the first sign of fall foliage, millions of monarch butterflies prep for an 8000-kilometre flight from southern Canada all the way down to central Mexico. Monarch butterflies return to Canada in spring to enjoy the budding flowers and share their piñatas with their Canadian friends.

Meat Feat

With 67.7 percent of the Canadian market, the province of Alberta is **Canada's Biggest Beef Producer.**

Excellent Stage Presence

Percheron horses have excellent stage presence—not on the theatrical stage, mind you. A hardy breed of draft horse, the commanding Percheron horse hails from France and is best known for pulling stagecoaches. The **World's Largest Herd of Percheron Horses** can be found at Bar U Ranch in Pekisko, Alberta, where they lead carriage tours throughout the historic grounds.

Sounds Greek to Me

Any Greek restaurant would be ecstatic to be in business with this next record holder. Weighing over 2.2 tonnes, the **World's Largest Atlantic Giant Squid** would supply enough calamari (deep-fried squid) to fill even Zeus' godly gut. Discovered on the shores of Thimble Tickle Bay near Glovers Harbour, Newfoundland and Labrador, on November 2, 1878, the torso of the sea creature measured seven metres in length, while its tentacles each stretched 11 metres in length. To give you a better understanding of just how massive this mollusc was, its tentacles were covered in suckers measuring 8.2 centimetres in diameter, and its eyeballs were the size of a full-grown human head. After its discovery, the carcass was chopped up and served to the local dog population. Today, a massive monument in honour of the giant squid can be found in Glovers Harbour.

Let's NOT Do Lunch

Don't ever agree to go on a dinner date with a polar bear. Not only are they bad tippers, but they might also eat you. The **Biggest Carnivore in Canada**, the polar bear is also the **World's Largest Meat-eater on Land**, as well as the **World's Largest Bear**.

Generally found in the frigid Canadian North, a polar bear eats mainly seals. With its white fur serving as camouflage in snow, a polar bear patiently waits next to a seal breathing hole in the ice. When a seal comes up for air, the polar bear uses a massive forepaw to pull its prey onto the ice.

Adult males weigh between 400 and 600 kilograms, so polar bears have a hearty appetite. Filling up on as many seals as they can before the summer thaw arrives, polar bears are then usually forced to go without food for several months until the ice, snow and seal population return.

Shrew World Order

If **Canada's Smallest Mammal** ruled the world, we'd all scurry through the grass and eat worms. Fortunately, the pygmy shrew has terrible eyesight, weighs 2.5 grams and is seven centimetres long, including its tail, so the likelihood of it ruling the world is pretty much nil.

Found throughout Canada, except for the colder parts up north, pygmy shrews are seldom seen by human eyes. They tend to live in forested areas, making their burrows under logs and in rocky crevices. However, if you ever do spot a pygmy shrew, stroke its ego a bit and pretend that you're afraid of it.

Basking in the Praise

It may seem that big fish tend to exist only in tall tales told by fishermen. But in the case of **Canada's Largest Fish**, the size is no exaggeration. The world's second largest fish after the whale shark, the basking shark is Canada's biggest fish. Found off the East Coast, the largest of the species was caught in a herring net in the Bay of Fundy in 1851. The total length of the basking shark measured a record-breaking 12.27 metres, and the behemoth weighed an estimated 17 tonnes. Known for its distinctive, net-like jaw, which can expand to one metre wide, the basking shark is considered a filter feeder, dredging the ocean with its enormous mouth, collecting plankton and filtering out the water. Able to grow to the length of a city bus, basking sharks are so monstrous that in centuries past, when one would wash up on shore, many people assumed that they were some type of sea serpent or a throwback to the dinosaurs.

Fish Feat

In September 2009, the **World's Largest Rainbow Trout** was caught in Saskatchewan's Lake Diefenbaker. The record-setting trout weighed approximately 22 kilograms.

Catch of the Century

Contrary to popular belief, tuna doesn't naturally come from tin cans. The bluefin variety of tuna is an ample aquatic creature that calls the Atlantic Ocean home and helped fisherman Ken Fraser set a world record. In 1979, off the coast of Nova Scotia, Fraser caught the **World's Heaviest Bluefin Tuna**. While on average, a bluefin tuna can weigh up to 350 kilograms, Fraser's bluefin tipped the scales at 680 kilograms. When hung up

by its tail, Fraser's bluefin was as long as two adult males are tall. Unfortunately, increasing demand by the sushi industry now threatens the mighty bluefin's survival.

Bragging Rights

Way to go, High Prairie, Alberta! For the last 21 years, you have staged **North American's Richest Fishing Tournament**. In September 2009 alone, the Golden Walleye Classic offered contestants $107,850 in prize money for the heaviest catch of the day.

Triple Threat

Who would have thought that a tiny reptile could hold one world record, let alone three? Believe it or not, a 300-million-year-old lizard, measuring 30 centimetres long, including its tail, is the **World's Oldest, Smallest and Earliest Fully Adapted Land Vertebrate**.

The remains of Hylonomus—as the creature was christened—were first uncovered near Horton Bluff, Nova Scotia, in 1851. Fossilized footprints belonging to Hylonomus have also been discovered in New Brunswick. Unfortunately, even though Hylonomus was a three-time world-record holder, because of his small size he was still picked last in gym class.

Jaw's Nightmare

If sharks slept like humans, then the **World's Largest Great White Shark** would give them nightmares. And who could blame them? On average, great white sharks range in length from six to 10 metres. This particular one, however, which was caught off New Brunswick's White Head Island during the 1930s, was 11.3 metres long. In those days, fishermen would extract the oil from the bellies of sharks for medicinal purposes, such as healing scars or abrasions. When the fisherman used this oil-extraction process on the record-setting swimmer, they removed over 1000 litres of oil—more than enough to heal just about any type of affliction, except for maybe a great white shark bite.

Fin Feat

In August 1961, the **World's Largest Lake Trout** was caught in Lake Athabasca, which lies on the Alberta-Saskatchewan border. The record-setting trout weighed approximately 46 kilograms!

Dog Is My Co-pilot

Everyone knows that a dog loves to stick its head out the window of a moving car. But very few dogs can actually roll down the window without human assistance—except for Striker. A brainy border collie from Québec City, Québec, Striker holds the world's record for the **Fastest Car Window Opened by a Dog**.

On September 1, 2004, Striker unwound a non-electric car window in 11.34 seconds. Now, all Striker needs to do is to learn how to work the gas pedal, and he and his friends can start car-pooling to obedience school.

Big Blowhole

Although Jonah and Geppetto managed to remain alive while inside a whale, if they had been trapped inside **Canada's Largest Aquatic Animal**, they would not only have survived, they could have fitted a Starbucks inside with them. Known to weigh more than 132 tonnes and measure 27 metres in length, the blue whale is one underwater whopper.

Every year, these whales, whose diet consists mainly of the tiny crustacean called krill, attract boatloads of whale watchers to the Gulf of Saint Lawrence, which is bordered by Québec, Newfoundland and Labrador, Prince Edward Island and Nova Scotia.

Thanks to a 1966 ban, it is illegal to hunt blue whales. Prior to the ban, the species was nearly hunted into extinction. And don't let anyone ever tell you that blue whales are insensitive creatures—these whales have the **Largest Heart of Any Living Animal** on earth, and the organ sometimes weighs up to 600 kilograms.

Octo-Momma Mia

If you're a glove manufacturer, you're going to love our next record holder. Found off the west coast of British Columbia, the North Pacific giant octopus is the **World's Largest Octopus**.

Proudly bearing eight spindly tentacles that can span up to seven metres in length, some North Pacific octopi can reach weights of up to 70 kilograms.

Sustaining itself on a healthy diet of shrimp, clams and fish, the North Pacific octopus is also on the menu of a number of ocean predators, including otters and whales. In the past, wrestling North Pacific octopi for sport was a popular pastime. At the 1963 World Octopus Wrestling Championships, 111 human contestants wrestled approximately 25 North Pacific octopi to shore. There is no confirmation, however, on the rumours that the octopi wore coloured spandex to their wrestling bouts.

Hoofing It

While Canada has spawned a number of the world's fastest humans, surprisingly, it has also given the world the **Second Fastest Animal**. Capable of reaching speeds of up to 100 kilometres per hour, the pronghorn antelope is **Canada's Fastest Animal**. It is bested in speed only by the cheetah, which can run up to 120 kilometres per hour. But, unlike the cheetah, the pronghorn antelope can sustain its velocity for a longer period of time. Found mostly in the grassland areas of southern Saskatchewan and Alberta, the pronghorn antelope can be recognized by the jagged set of horns that protrude from its forehead. These horns can be a real pain in the butt, if allowed to ram your butt at full speed.

King of the Plains

When you're the **Largest Land Animal Native to Canada**, you can pretty much go wherever you want and not get hassled. Case in point—the North American buffalo, or bison, as they're known in Canada. With a mature male capable of reaching a whopping 1090 kilograms in weight, 3.9 metres in length and 1.8 metres in height, bison are extremely formidable mammals. Fortunately for humans, they are herbivores, eating only the plant life that they come across while foraging across the Canadian Prairies. Although the species was hunted nearly to extinction, today Canada's wild bison is a protected species that has been steadily increasing in numbers.

Sweet Feat

With 25,000 beehives, Falher, Alberta, is home to **Canada's Biggest Honey Farm**, which, on average, produces two million kilograms of honey per year.

Tusk 'til Dawn

Elephants, like everyone else, like to have a perfect smile. So when Spike, the Calgary Zoo's resident Asian pachyderm, cracked his tusks, he had to make a dental appointment. But this was more than just an average visit to the dentist—this was a record-setting operation. On July 4, 2002, Spike's fractured tusks were fitted with the **World's Largest Dental Caps**. Designed at the Southern Alberta Institute of Technology from stainless steel, the caps measured 50 centimetres long, 13 centimetres around and weighed 13 kilograms each. The surgery took a total of three hours and 30 minutes to complete. And although Spike was pleased with the results, he wasn't so pleased with the dentist's bill.

Dumbosaur

Dinosaurs weren't known for their brains; however, one specific "thunder lizard" was so stupid that it holds the title of **Dumbest Creature to Roam Canada**.

Well-recognized for its plated back and spiked tail, the *Stegosaurus* wasn't the brightest dinosaur to meander the Alberta badlands during the Late Jurassic period. With a brain that weighed about 80 grams--similar to the weight of a dog's brain--the *Stegosaurus* is considered to have had the smallest brain of any dinosaur. However, seeing that they measured nine metres in length, four metres in height and had nearly impenetrable defensive body amour, calling a Stegosaurus an idiot would certainly make you one as well.

All You Can Leap

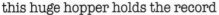

Forget the "ribbit" sound that most frogs make— this ample amphibian just croaked for more riblets. Discovered near Killarney Lake, New Brunswick, in 1885, this huge hopper holds the record for the **World's Fattest Frog**. Raised on a steady diet of bugs, bread, beer and buttermilk, this voluptuous vertebrate tipped the scales at an improbable 19 kilograms. Widely known as the Coleman Frog, it was named after Fred Coleman, an area hotel owner who frequently fed the creature. The frog was considered by many people to be a rural legend, until the day that its dead body was discovered. Upon its death, Coleman displayed the flabby frog's girth in the lobby of his hotel for all to see. While some say the Coleman Frog died in an explosion designed to flush fish out of the lake, clogged arteries could have also contributed to the amphibian's demise.

Oh, Deer

Along with beavers and tooth-less hockey players, the moose is a Canadian icon, so it's no wonder that a homegrown moose holds the record for the **World's Largest Deer**. In the fall of 1897, near the Yukon River, a hunter shot an Alaska moose that weighed a record-breaking 816 kilograms. In its prime, the moose was 2.3 metres tall at the shoulder. No other moose has even come close to breaking the record—or else it has been smart enough to avoid being shot by a hunter.

Bragging Rights

Congratulations, Québec! You have the **Most Dairy Cows of any Canadian Province**. In fact, your "udderly" amazing herds make up 40 percent of the total number of Canadian dairy cows.

The Predictable Whistle Pig

Whistle pigs, woodchucks or groundhogs—no matter what you call them, these varmints are the reason behind the inclusion of Wiarton, Ontario, in the record books. For over 40 years, the Wiarton Willie Festival, held every February 2 in the community of Wiarton, has been recognized as the **Largest Groundhog Festival in Canada**.

Centred around a weather-predicting albino groundhog named Willie, the festival is Canada's best opportunity to find out if there will be an early spring or a long, long winter. Every February 2, Willie exited his borrow, and if he didn't see his shadow, spring would soon arrive. However, after prognosticating the weather for 22 years—the **Longest Lifespan of Any Known Groundhog**—Wiarton Willie passed away in 1999. Fortunately, Wee Willie, Willie's offspring, has followed in his famous father's forecasting footprints. For the record, a groundhog's accuracy in correctly predicting the onset of spring is about 37 percent, which means if Willie senior and junior were being paid for their forecasting abilities, both would have been fired a long time ago.

Bragging Rights

Sold! To Ponoka, Alberta's annual stampede—the home of **Canada's Largest Single-day Livestock Auction**.

The Finest Fleece

Bye-bye, baa, baa, black sheep—no one's going to want your wool after they hear about the mighty muskox. Found on Banks Island, Northwest Territories, and elsewhere in the Arctic, this distant cousin of the wild sheep and goat is considered to have the **Warmest Wool in the World**. The underwool, which the Inuit call qiviut, is in high demand for its malleability and insulative qualities. Be warned, however, if you're thinking about knitting yourself a qiviut coat—you will pay anywhere from $40 to $80 per 28 grams of the underwool, so why not knit a pair of qiviut socks instead?

Animal Testing

1. Which of the following is the most popular cat breed in Canada?
    A. Himalayan
    B. Persian
    C. Tabby
    D. Fat

2. Which of the following is the most popular dog breed in Canada?
    A. Golden retriever
    B. Shih tzu
    C. Labrador
    D. Talking

3. Which of the following is the most-caught species of fish in Canada?
    A. Trout
    B. Walleye
    C. Perch
    D. Mermaid

Answers on page 239.

Animal Rescue

This country's finest fauna have contracted amnesia and have lost their way: lobsters are hailing cabs in Alberta, while polar bears are visiting Peggy's Cove. As Canada's most daring animal wrangler, it is your job to locate this wayward wildlife and return each animal to its correct region, safe and sound.

Nova Scotia	Pronghorn
Newfoundland	Bobcat
Saskatchewan	Red fox
Manitoba	Orca
British Columbia	Flying squirrel
Alberta	Polar Bear
Ontario	Mountain goat
Québec	Lobster
Prince Edward Island	Wild boar
New Brunswick	Caribou
Northwest Territories	Beluga
Yukon	Puffin
Nunavut	Moose

Answers on page 239.

Bewildered Beasts

While on their way to the Calgary Zoo, a cargo full of critters for the zoo's new exhibit got scrambled in transit and forgot which animals they were. Now, as the zoo's top animal psychiatrist, it is your job to talk and listen to the animals and help them remember their animalistic traits before the exhibit opens.

SLEAEW _____

LAES _____

BCIARUO _____

OMMRAT _____

BBCOAT _____

OYOECT _____

SNUKK _____

ELOV _____

EONWRIVLE _____

AESKN _____

RSLWUA _____

NBOIS _____

LEK _____

CKIMNPUH _____

COKUHODWC _____

ORGUAC _____

AEHLW _____

OKSMUX _____

PETLONEA _____

Answers on page 239.

The _____est Beasts

Animal Crossing

While visiting Marineland Canada in Niagara Falls, Ontario, you and three other audience members were chosen to ride on the back of a dolphin. Unfortunately, there is only enough time for one person to go. And that person will be whoever completes the following crossword the fastest.

ACROSS

1. Bird ancestor
3. Says no to gills
4. Bear's break
7. Cold blooded
9. Night owl
10. Home to Charlotte
11. Shows backbone
13. Eats meat and vegetables

DOWN

2. Multi-limbed spinner
3. Primate cousin
4. Pet shop top seller
5. Eggs' place
6. Sweater predecessor
8. Black Beauty or Flicka
10. Prison to Fido
12. Canines

Answers on page xxx.

Word Safari

Someone opened all the cages at the zoo last night, and all the animals escaped into a nearby forest. Now, as the zoo's top tortoise cleaner, it is your job to head into that forest and locate the animals listed below.

```
R M M I B W D I C R S O X O F Y D B M B C
E N R O H G N O R P Q O W C B E I A U I H
E A C B R E E S H O U M S K I K N C S R W
D H M U S K R A T H I C D E R R S O R D S
O L G P D I K R O B R S R L K U E W K S T
O Y B S G O R F O E R B A T S T C I A U U
L N D R V W K Y N A E X Z W H Y T R R N G
N X Y B A G R W C V L O I D O W S T L L N
R E S E E E A Z C A P D L R L S L E P D I
A R R C V Q H E D R K C U D P E N A M B M
B A K A O S S H W B I T E Q G Q M O O C M
B V E Z X I E U S R A C C O O N O M O S E
I B O R O R Y N T O M D K S F V E R S Z L
T S H P I G U R E H P O G R G E A S E W O
S C R C B R R O J K T S W E N E K C I H C
A O S T P O L A R B E A R E R A H N O U D
P Y X L W O C W E G G R O U N D H O G N W
```

Porpoise	Muskrat	Chicken
Pronghorn	Gopher	Squirrel
Lizard	Cow	Deer
Raccoon	Pig	Beaver
Fox	Owl	Moose
Lemming	Rabbits	Polar Bear
Badger	Turtle	Frogs
Hare	Shark	Birds
Bat	Groundhog	Insects
Lynx	Turkey	Duck

The _____est Beasts

The _____est Landscape

Deepest	Loveliest
Craggiest	Flattest
Greenest	Grassiest
Iciest	Saltiest
Starkest	Ugliest
Highest	Lowest
Remotest	Harshest
Richest	Hilliest

(Superlative recommendations for chapter
title—pick one or add your own)

Insane Terrain

To paint a proper portrait of Canada, you will need the darkest colour of green to capture our bountiful forests, a silvery tint to recreate our craggy mountaintops, azure blue to embody our oceans, creamy white to capture the stark chill of our winter snowfall and golden yellow to exemplify our sandy beaches. In short, to accurately depict Canada, you'll need every hue, tone and shade of colour imaginable. The second largest country in the world, after Russia, Canada is the only country that encompasses just about every type of land formation there is—mountains, hills, rainforests, whirlpools, prairies, glaciers, icebergs, lakes, streams, deserts, frozen waste-lands and waterfalls. Canada is tops in topography.

Not surprisingly, people from around the world travel to see this country's natural beauty, swim in its temperate waters, ski its snow-capped mountains and explore its massive icefields.

But Canada's terrain is not only for tourists to take photos of, it is also imperative to our way of life. Prince Edward Island's red soil gives us some of the plumpest potatoes around, while the Hudson Bay Lowlands teem with crude oil, and reclaimed ocean in New Brunswick serves as the some of the most fertile agricultural land fathomable.

This land may belong to you and me, but Canadians, along with Australian ski-bums, Japanese tourists and American oil companies, all owe a debt of gratitude to this _____est landscape.

Nerd Alert

Considered **Canada's Smartest City**, Kingston, Ontario, is a school bully's paradise. With a population of around 152,360, more than 2500 of those residents have earned doctorates. This means that 1.67 percent of Kingston's population holds a PhD, the most of any major Canadian city. Because of this high concentration of braniacs, the national headquarters of the world's largest and oldest high-IQ society, MENSA, calls Kingston home.

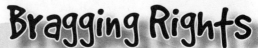

Bragging Rights

Big up, T-Dot! You're not only **Canada's Largest City**, but you are its **Most Populated City** as well. Consisting of an area measuring approximately 630 square kilometres, with a population in excess of 2.5 million, Toronto would feel at home to sardines.

Mount Ka-Booom!

What's the best way to deal with a pesky underwater mountain peak that juts out of the water at low tide, creating whirlpools and tearing the bottoms out of passing transport vessels?

You annihilate it in the **World's Largest Intentional Non-nuclear Peacetime Explosion**, that's what you do.

"One of the vilest stretches of water in the world," is how explorer Captain George Vancouver described Seymour Narrows. The narrows lie north of Campbell River, British Columbia, between Quadra Island and Vancouver Island,

and straddle the submerged mountain known as Ripple Rock, which had been a thorn in the side of many a sailor for more than 75 years. Then, on April 5, 1958—after the National Research Council of Canada spent over two years tunnelling into the crag and cramming it with more than 1200 tonnes of explosives—Ripple Rock went from sitting three metres below the surface to being submerged 14 metres underwater. The record-setting blast sent 635,000 tonnes of debris flying 300 metres in all directions. On hand to broadcast the momentous mountain decapitation was the CBC, in what turned out to be the network's first-ever live national broadcast.

Bragging Rights

You're it, Canada! You have the **Longest and Straightest International Border in the World**. Known as the 49th parallel, this lengthy line of latitude extends across the bottom portion of the country for an astounding 2043 kilometres, separating us (Canada) from U.S. (America).

Feeling Brine

When visiting Watrous, Saskatchewan, if you have high blood pressure, you may not want to go swimming in Manitou Lake—**Canada's Saltiest Lake**.

With three times more salt than the Dead Sea, Manitou Lake is ideal for non-swimmers, because the high salinity results in extreme buoyancy, making it virtually impossible for a person to sink. But the lake's ability to levitate swimmers is not its only magic trick. Plains Natives used to bring their sick and old to the shores of Manitou Lake because the waters were thought to have healing powers. The water's medicinal benefits led to its widespread nickname "the Lake of Good Spirit." Unfortunately, there is a downside to the lake's power. The abundance of salt in the water makes it impossible for Manitou Lake to sustain any wildlife, so cancel that fishing trip.

Sightseeing

When in Cypress Hills, I spy with my little eye, the **Highest Point of Land in Saskatchewan**—1468 metres above sea level.

Extreme Long Walks on the Beach

If you are looking for a romantic walk on a beach, you may not want to go to Wasaga Beach, Ontario, because it will seem like you are walking forever. Considered the **World's Longest Freshwater Beach**, Wasaga is located two hours north of downtown Toronto on Lake Huron's Nottawasaga Bay. The white sand beach, which stretches 14 kilometres east to west, is divided into a number of smaller public beaches. In summer, Wasaga is a mecca to sun worshippers. In winter, it is a frozen fantasyland for cross-country skiers and snowmobile enthusiasts.

Long Feat

Encompassing over 386 kilometres of lakes, rivers, locks and canals from Lake Ontario to Georgian Bay, the Trent-Severn Waterway is **Canada's Longest Historic Site**.

Spin Cycle

You may get a little queasy hearing about our next wonder, so don't eat lunch until after reading. Dubbed "Old Sow" because of the swine-like noise it produces, this powerful puddle of whirling water, located between Passamaquoddy Bay and the Bay of Fundy, west of Deer Island, New Brunswick, is the **Western Hemisphere's Largest Tidal Whirlpool**.

With a diameter of 76 metres, the vortex is recognized as one of the **Top-Five Most Significant Whirlpools in the World**. The result of a large amount of seawater being pushed into the western passageway, where it swirls around like an underwater tornado, the current inside the Old Sow can reach speeds of up to 28 kilometres per hour. Currently, Old Sow is tied with a whirlpool in Norway as the **World's the Most Powerful Whirlpool**.

Bragging Rights

That's what I'm talking about! Even though it shares the honour with the United States, Lake Michigan-Huron is still **Canada's Largest Freshwater Lake**, with an area of 117,702 square kilometres.

How Low Can You Go?

When someone says that Great Slave Lake is really deep, they're not talking about how intellectually complex

The _____est Landscape

it is, they're talking about its physical depth. Formed by a retreating glacier over 10,000 years ago, Great Slave Lake in the Northwest Territories is 614 metres deep, which makes it **Canada's Deepest Lake** and the **Second Largest Lake in Canada**, after Great Bear Lake. On a global scale, GSL is the ninth largest and the sixth deepest lake in the world.

And don't worry about its moniker—the name Great Slave Lake has nothing to do with slavery; it was named after the Slavey people, who inhabited its shores.

Two feat

With a size of 497 square kilometres and a length of 177 kilometres, Babine Lake is the **Largest and Longest Natural Lake in British Columbia**.

Unbearably Big

Canada has numerous lakes, but none of them are as ferocious as Great Bear Lake—the **Largest Lake Completely Inside Canada's Borders**. To clarify, both Lake Superior and Lake Huron are larger than Great Bear Lake, but neither of them lies entirely within the borders of Canada.

Located in the Northwest Territories, Great Bear Lake has a surface area of 31,153 square kilometres and a depth of 71.7 metres. But don't pack your beach blanket and swim trunks just yet. Since the lake is located on the Arctic Circle, it is covered with ice and snow from November to

July. And even when the ice does melt, the water temperature of Great Bear Lake reaches a maximum of only around 12°C. Brrrr! Sounds like it should change its name to Great Polar Bear Lake.

Sightseeing

When looking at Lake Superior, I spy with my little eye, the **Canadian Lake with the Greatest Volume of Water**—12,174 cubic kilometres.

Score-osaurus

If you are ever interested in seeing what became of Earth's mightiest predators—the dinosaurs—then look no farther than your car's gas tank. Widely known as a popular prehistoric party place, the province of Alberta not only has a good portion of the world's oil, but is also the **World's Richest Area of Dinosaur Fossils**.

In the valley of the Red Deer River, northeast of Brooks, near the heart of Alberta's badlands, stands Dinosaur Provincial Park. Established in 1955, the park is a hotbed of thunder-lizard fossils. An amazing 40 different dinosaur species have been discovered inside the World Heritage Site, along with a number of fossilized plants. The park's most significant dino-score was the discovery of fossils belonging to a Champsosaurus, an alligator-like creature that hunted throughout the Red Deer River area over a million years ago.

The _____est Landscape

Big Feat

With a massive measurement of 1,542,056 square kilometres, Québec is **Canada's Largest Province.**

Metal Mayhem

If you're a werewolf and would like to stay that way, make sure that you never visit Cobalt, Ontario. Mystical creatures susceptible to the power of the precious metal will definitely feel uneasy in **Ontario's Most Historic Town**, which was also the home of the **World's Richest Vein of Silver**.

During the construction of the Temiskaming and Northern Ontario Railway in 1903, a pure vein of silver was discovered. Filled with dreams of getting rich—filthy rich, I tell's ya—prospectors from all over descended upon Cobalt and worked the mines until the silver was depleted, which occurred sometime in the 1930s.

In 1911, during the area's heyday, the production of silver in Cobalt was greater than 30 million ounces. And although the "Silver Age" didn't last forever, it did leave an indelible mark on the town, which christened its National Hockey Association team the Cobalt Silver Kings.

Rock of Ages

Q: What does an ancient rock call its grandchildren?

A: Sandchildren.

If you don't believe me, just ask the Acasta Gneiss (pronounced "nice")—the **Oldest Rock in Canada**. About four billion years old, the senior stone juts out of the ground east of Great Bear Lake, Northwest Territories. Considered to be the **Oldest Known Exposed Rock in the World**, Acasta Gneiss was once a fragment of the earth's crust.

Sightseeing

While swimming near Bowie Seamount, British Columbia, I spy with my little eye, the **Tallest Underwater Mountain in Canadian Waters**—3000 metres high and 20 metres below the surface of the Pacific Ocean.

Canada's Hottest Bod

You won't find Canada's hottest body on the silver screen or in a magazine; you'll find it in Gladstone Provincial Park, British Columbia, home of **Canada's Warmest Lake**, Christina Lake. Throughout the months of July and August, the temperature of this hot body of water can reach 24°C to 25°C—and that's before swimmers have a chance to pee in it.

Bragging Rights

How refreshing! Tchesinkut Lake has the **Purest Water in British Columbia**. Its very name means "clear waters."

Salted Feat

Covering an area of 1100 square kilometres, Nova Scotia's Bras d'Or Lake is the **World's Largest Saltwater Lake.**

Junk in the Trunk

With a trunk measuring almost five metres in diameter, **Saskatchewan's Largest Tree** is so big that it makes the province seem like it has scenery.

Just kidding, Saskatchewan, you're beautiful—don't ever change.

Growing outside Blaine Lake, Saskatchewan, for more than 160 years, this colossal cottonwood–balsam polar hybrid has gangly branches that droop from its trunk like a set of timber tentacles. Stretching skyward for nearly 21 vertical metres, the once-larger tree had its top fried off by lightning during an electrical storm. Nevertheless, for a tree, being hit by lightning sure beats being chopped down by a lumberjack and turned into a toothpick or a phone book.

Sightseeing

When in Point Pelee, Ontario, I spy with my little eye, the **Most Southerly Point in Mainland Canada.**

Branching Out

You don't want to get your kite stuck up in this next tall piece of timber. Standing a whopping 96 metres tall, the Carmanah Giant is **Canada's Largest Tree**. Growing in Vancouver Island's Carmanah Walbran Provincial Park, the super-sized Sitka spruce is nestled in a deep ravine, which keeps it protected from the harsh elements. Height isn't the mighty conifer's only attribute, however. The tree is also estimated to be a little over 400 years old. But if you ask me, the Carmanah Giant doesn't look a day over 375.

Bragging Rights

Ice move, Columbia Icefield! You're the **World's Largest Non-Polar Ice Cap**. Straddling the border between British Columbia and Alberta, the Columbia Icefield covers 325 square kilometres. It also has a depth of nearly 300 metres.

Ice Cubed

Comedian: The Largest Iceberg in the Northern Hemisphere was so large...

Audience: How large was it?

Comedian: It was so large that it towered 20 metres above the water's surface.

Audience: Boo! Get off the stage!

The _____est Landscape

Comedian: How about the fact that the iceberg was made of so much ice...

Audience: How much ice was it made of?

Comedian: It was made of so much ice that if were melted down, there would be enough liquid runoff to give everyone in the entire world a litre of water to drink, every day, for approximately four years.

Audience: Intriguing—tell us more.

Comedian: The iceberg was first discovered off the coast of Baffin Island, **Canada's Largest Island**, in 1882, and measured 13 kilometres long and six kilometres wide.

Audience: Learning is fun.

Comedian: Thank you, you've been a great audience.

Little Feat

With a diminutive size of 5683.91 square kilometres, Prince Edward Island is **Canada's Smallest Province**.

H_2O, Yeah

If Lake Huron's Manitoulin Island ever gets fresh with you, don't worry—that's its claim to fame. Covering an area of approximately 2766 kilometres, Manitoulin Island is the **Largest Freshwater Island in the World**. Considered to be a sacred place by early First Nations peoples, the island's name is from the Ojibwa language and means "Spirit Island."

Sightseeing

When in Sandbanks Provincial Park, Ontario, I spy with my little eye, the **World's Largest Freshwater Sandbar and Dune System**.

Newfound Glory

Becoming the 10th province to join Canada, in 1949, Newfoundland holds the distinction of being the **Youngest Province in Canada**, although, technically, it's even younger than that. In fact, it was only in 2001 that Newfoundland and Labrador amalgamated into one new province. Besides youth, the Rock has location, location, location on its side. Situated on the tip of the country's East Coast, Newfoundland is the **Most Easterly Province in Canada**. What's more, it's the only Canadian province to have its own provincial dog, the Labrador. Stranger still, there are no frogs, porcupines, snakes or skunks to be found at large anywhere within the borders of Newfoundland.

Sightseeing

When in Cape St. Charles, Newfoundland and Labrador, I spy with my little eye, the **Most Easterly Point in Mainland Canada**.

The _____est Landscape

Green Thumbs Up

Surprisingly, **Canada's Richest Garden Market** doesn't get its title because it grows money on trees. It gets its name by producing some of the finest vegetables and flowers for the domestic marketplace. Planted in Bradford, Ontario, the fertile patch of land was once a section of glacial Lake Algonquin. That is, before the marshland was drained in the late 1920s. When the swamp water was finally evacuated from the quagmire, a 150-metre-deep deposit of rotting vegetation was uncovered. Rich in minerals, the soil under the vegetation was ideal for agriculture. Unfortunately, however, the mineral-rich soil was insufficient for the cultivation of money trees.

Sightseeing

When in Canada, I spy with my little eye, the **Second Largest Country in the World**.

Swamp Meet

Rubber boots and an extra pair of dry socks are essential when visiting the **World's Largest Wetland**. Sandwiched between the Canadian Shield and the southern shores of Hudson Bay and James Bay, the Hudson Bay Lowlands take up a soggy area of approximately 300,000 square kilometres. The boggy backdrop is the result of poor drainage and provides a haven for millions of blackflies and blood-sucking mosquitoes. However, those pesky wee beasties are no match for the oil companies—the Lowlands are loaded with precious oil deposits.

Sightseeing

When in Great Sand Hills west of Swift Current, Saskatchewan, I spy with my little eye, the **Largest Uninterrupted Area of Sand Dunes in Southern Canada**—1911 square kilometres.

Potash Stash

If I were to tell you where the **World's Largest Potash Mine** could be found, you'd probably say, "What the heck is potash?" Then I'd probably respond, "It's potassium carbonate, a type of salt that is found in the earth and used as a fertilizer." And even though you'd want me to stop, I'd continue saying something else like, "The largest potash mine is found in Esterhazy, Saskatchewan, and produces 3.8 million tonnes of fertilizer per year, making Saskatchewan the **World's Largest Exporter of Potash**." Now aren't you glad you asked about potash?

Peak Feat

At 3363 metres high, Mount Edith Cavell is the **Tallest Peak in Jasper National Park, Alberta**.

The _____est Landscape

A Serious Summit

As any mountain goat can tell you, Mount Logan, located in the southwest Yukon, is the **Highest Peak in Canada**. Unfortunately, if you don't speak mountain goat, then you'll just have to take my word for it. Discovered in 1890 by W.E. Logan, founder of the Geological Survey of Canada, Mount Logan's peak is 5959 metres above sea level. Believed to have the **Largest Base Circumference of Any Non-Volcanic Mountain** on Earth, the massif (a compact group of mountains) consists of 11 peaks over 5000 metres in height. What's more, its three summits form the **World's Largest Alpine Massif**. And, thanks to continual tectonic activity underneath the mountain range, Mount Logan's elevation is continually increasing.

Sightseeing

On top of Mount Caubvick in New-foundland and Labrador (a.k.a. Mont d'Iberville in Québec), I spy with my little eye, the **Highest Mountain in Atlantic Canada**—1652 metres elevation.

Mountains, Man

When you're the **Oldest National Park in Canada**, you get to eat off the seniors' menu. Discovered by chance in 1883 by railway workers Frank McCabe and brothers

William and Tom McCardell, Banff was established as a national park two years later. Nestled in the Alberta Rockies, Banff is world renowned for its skiing, sulphur hot springs and glaciers. It's also home to a metre-long, petrified half-man, half-fish creature known as the Merman, which can be found in the back of the Indian Trading Post.

Two Provinces for the Price of One

Lloydminster is extremely popular. Like a fair maiden caught between two potential suitors, it lies across the Saskatchewan-Alberta border, making it the titleholder of the **Most Provinces in One City**.

With its main street located on the 110th parallel, Lloydminster is split down the middle. All the residents on one side of 50th Avenue live in Saskatchewan, while all the residents on the other side live in Alberta. Even the city's flag reflects the provincial divide, sporting both an Alberta wild rose and a Saskatchewan western red lily. However, wouldn't designating Lloydminster as its own province be a lot easier than having it be a part of two provinces? I suggest this new province be called Sasberta.

Sightseeing

When in Moraine Lake, Banff National Park, Alberta, I spy with my little eye, the **Most Photographed Lake in the World**.

Monster Marsh

Although they weren't assembled out of stray body parts in the laboratory of a mad scientist, the Tantramar Marshes are a monstrous sight to behold. Occupying an area of approximately 202 square kilometres, the marshes make up the **World's Biggest Hayfield**. Located on the eastern tip of New Brunswick, the swampland became farmland in the 1770s, when Acadian settlers set up a system of dikes to hold the seawater back. Rich with minerals, the newly claimed land has become the hotspot for hay production over the last two centuries. The marshes' peculiar name was inspired by the noise that the local waterfowl made—"tantramar" is the Acadian word for "racket."

Sheer Feat

With a 350-metre plunge, Pissing Mare Falls in Gros Morne National Park, Newfoundland and Labrador, is **Eastern North America's Highest Waterfall**.

The Tide is Right

As we know, the moon not only regulates the lifecycle of werewolves, it also manipulates the tides. And there are no tides more controlled by gravitational pull than the Bay of Fundy, which has the **World's Highest Tides**. Situated on the Atlantic Coast between New Brunswick and Nova Scotia, the bay boasts a difference between its low and high tides that can be up to 16 metres. The Bay of Fundy was recently short-listed as a finalist for the New Seven Wonders of Nature. The selection of the seven will be finalized in 2011.

Sightseeing

When on Prince Edward Island, I spy with my little eye, the **Largest Island on the East Coast of Canada**, excluding the Arctic Islands.

Waterfalling in Love

Yes, Virginia Falls, Canada does have a **Largest Vertical Stream of Water**, and you're it. With a face measuring 1.6 hectares, a vertical drop of 90 metres and an annual discharge of 1000 cubic metres per second, Virginia Falls, Northwest Territories, is **Canada's Largest Waterfall**. Although twice as high as Niagara Falls, Virginia Falls doesn't measure up when it comes to the tallest falls. The title of **Canada's Tallest Falls** usually falls to British Columbia's Della Falls, but other contenders are vying to be recognized. With a vertical drop of 440 metres and an annual discharge of 6000 cubic metres every second, Della Falls, located in Strathcona Provincial Park on Vancouver Island, are only accessible by boat or helicopter.

Sightseeing

When in Cape Spear on the Avalon Peninsula, Newfoundland and Labrador, I spy with my little eye, the **Most Easterly Point in North America**.

Bragging Rights

Great latitude, Cape Columbia, Nunavut! You're **Canada's Most
Northerly Point**. Located on the shores
of the Lincoln Sea in the Arctic Ocean, Cape
Columbia is considered to be one of the most
remote places in the world. So, unfortunately, there
aren't many people to brag about this
accomplishment to.

Go to Halifax

The next time someone tells you to go straight to Halifax—
do it. Not only is Halifax the home of **North America's
Largest Fishery**, it's also the **World's Largest Producer
of Lobsters, Christmas Trees and Wild Blueberries**.

Water-Winging It

Non-swimmers, rejoice!
At only 92.9 metres deep,
Hudson Bay, the **Larg-
est Body of Water in
Northeastern Canada**
is also the **Shallowest
Sea in Canada**.

Sightseeing

When looking at Chilko Lake, British
Columbia, I spy with my little eye, **Canada's
Highest Major Lake Over 100 Square
Kilometres in Area**—area 158 square kilo-
metres, elevation 1171 metres.

Land Minds

1. Which region of Canada has the smallest number of lakes over three square kilometres in size?
   A. British Columbia
   B. The Prairies
   C. Ontario
   D. The Maritimes

2. What is Canada's largest national park?
   A. Jasper National Park
   B. Fundy National Park
   C. Wood Buffalo National Park
   D. Wet Willy's Water Park

3. Where can you find the world's strongest current?
   A. Rustico, Prince Edward Island
   B. Slingsby Channel, British Columbia
   C. Hamstead, New Brunswick
   D. Swift Current, Saskatchewan

4. What is Canada's longest river?
   A. Yukon River
   B. Mackenzie River
   C. St. Lawrence River
   D. Amazon River

The _____est Landscape

5. What is the world's largest bay?
   A. Bay of Fundy
   B. Bombay
   C. Hudson Bay
   D. Green Bay   **Answers on page 240.**

Continental Drifting

Tectonic plates have shifted, displacing of a number of Canadian geological features from their original locations. Now, as a junior park warden, it is your job to round up these lost landscapes and return them to their rightful regions.

Alberta	Rankin Inlet
Prince Edward Island	Great Slave Lake
Newfoundland and Labrador	Badlands
New Brunswick	Red Soil
British Columbia	Churchill River
Yukon	Bay of Fundy
Manitoba	Sable Island
Ontario	Saint Lawrence River
Saskatchewan	Mount Logan
Nova Scotia	Giant Douglas-firs
Québec	Cypress Hills
Northwest Territories	Niagara Falls
Nunavut	Red River

Answers on page 240.

Landmass Destruction

A terrible earthquake has come along and mixed up a number of Canadian geography terms. As a geologist's assistant, it is your job to sort out the wreckage and put the letters in their correct order before the next after-shock hits.

NTOMUNAI _____

LYVELA _____

OTINELVEA _____

DGLONUITE _____

EDUIATLT _____

EDESGER _____

ERIRV _____

AEKL _____

PORILOWHL _____

REGAN _____

DFLEI _____

CERKE _____

YAB _____

IAUFQRE _____

EPOCAHGLIAR _____

LTAOL _____

HAERPOYGG _____

IAXS _____

OKBRO _____

KCOR _____

Answers on page 240.

Across Canada

You have the opportunity to be the King of Canada for one day. However, you must first complete the following topography-related crossword.

ACROSS
1. North America, for one
2. Western, for one
4. Low-lying land
6. Solid rock or home to the Flintstones
7. Cape Breton or Manitoulin
9. Ice Age leftover
11. Arid locale
13. Beaver, moose and goose
15. Where fresh and salt water mix

DOWN
1. Peggy's, for one
2. Central part of a region
3. Bush synonym
4. A weak point
5. Cleaner word for "dirt"
8. Found at the mouth of a river
10. Place locator
12. Poplar, for one
14. Similar to "bay"

Answers on page 240.

Land of the Lost Words

Flying over the Rockie Mountains on their way to a soccer game in Vancouver, the landscape-related words below crash-landed on the rocky range. Now, as a mountain rescue team member, it is your job to fly the helicopter over the peaks and locate the words.

```
B U S R D S L A G O O N P E O C N V E A F
A R D N U T O S E D I M E N T R O O L P U
E E R E G O O D F E N S D R P U Y L I L S
E H T S R C G N F R E I I F E S A C M A T
G I G T E R K A E P D V M F A E P A E I A
S L O W B U E L D C L E E W A R D N S N C
T L O E E S R D O R E D N L E E R E T S A
L C N T C T B A U U Q A T E P U E T O U Y
A E Y D I S L B P E Q U A T O R T I N C E
R I E R E E U O E N L V E E R E S Y E G I
P L N E R R N E F O R E S T L N U W E O R
E U A Q A A F H A B I T A N T I E E T R I
G F E U C D U U T Y L N R A E T T T P G A
B F C L E Q F Q A E L U E Y A E F R I E R
I B O R E A L M R O I L F G N L O L E A P
N V E A R F C A N Y O N O F E N R A Y F E
S A D N A L T E W A R E N E R I V E R E R
```

Volcano	Levee	Iceberg	River
Tundra	Limestone	Bluff	Site
Badlands	Geyser	Boreal	Crust
Sediment	Hill	Plains	Forest
Quarry	Equator	Canyon	Prairie
Peak	Fertile	Inlet	Wetland
Pediment	Gorge	Lagoon	
Leeward	Habitant	Ocean	

The _____ est Landscape

The _____est Athletes

Craziest	*Healthiest*
Richest	*Quickest*
Classiest	*Shallowest*
Liveliest	*Phoniest*
Lamest	*Whiniest*
Oldest	*Greatest*
Laziest	*Funniest*
Angriest	*Smelliest*
Fattest	*Wackiest*

(Superlative recommendations for chapter title—pick one or add your own)

Winners and Lugers

Canadians are active people, mostly because they must keep their blood from coagulating in the frigid climate. And while there's no doubt that Canucks excel at sports that pertain to frozen water and snowy slopes, we also bring our "eh" game to the summer sports. World-record holders for the longest baseball game and the longest street hockey game, as well as numerous swimming and lacrosse records, Canadians are all-season MVPs.

And it doesn't even have to be organized sports for us to show our dominance. We hold world records for walking, running, water-skiing, rowing and Pilates. What's more, some of our country's greatest record holders are old enough to be great-great-grandmothers and great-great-grandfathers, with some of our elderly athletes in excess of 100 years old.

On the opposite end, we have had a host of minors that have broken world records, including 16-year-old Marilyn Bell, who swam the English Channel, and Elaine Tanner, 15-year-old recipient of the Lou Marsh Trophy.

Young or old, hot or cold, Canadians eat sports records as part of a well-balanced breakfast, and it shows. Donovan Bailey, Wayne Gretzky and Gilles Villeneuve were all the best in their respective sports, and all called Canada home. Even our animals are contenders—for example, Northern Dancer, the most influential race-horse to ever hit the track. Canadians are so awesome

The _____est Athletes

*that we even mix it up and occasionally have humans,
like Tom Longboat, race against horses.*

But, regardless of all of that, the best part about Canadians and competition is, no matter if we win or lose, Canadians are always good sports. Game on!

Skiing is Believing

Just call them slope dopes. In 1986, Dave Phillips and Gary O'Neil of Vancouver, British Columbia, shredded North Vancouver's Grouse Mountain for an unprecedented 83 hours and 17 minutes straight—the **World's Longest Nonstop Ski**.

What the Puck!

The **World's Longest NHL Game** took place in 1936 between Montréal and Detroit in game one of the semi-final round of the Stanley Cup playoffs. They played 116 minutes of overtime, and the game finally ended when Detroit's Mud Bruneteau scored the game's only goal in the sixth overtime period after 176 minutes and 30 seconds of game play.

Hats Off to Billy

When you're in the presence of hockey legend Billy Mosienko, please remove all headwear and toss it at his feet. On March 23, 1952, the right-winger for the Chicago Black Hawks scored three goals against the New York Rangers in

21 seconds—the **NHL's Fastest Hat Trick**. Born in Winnipeg, Manitoba, on November 2, 1921, Mosienko played for the Black Hawks for 14 seasons. In 1965, he was inducted into the Hockey Hall of Fame for his record-setting feat, which still stands to this day. Also still standing is a five-and-10-pin bowl-a-rama in Winnipeg named after the hometown hero. So it would appear that Mosienko may have also been interested in breaking the **World's Fastest Turkey** (three consecutive strikes in bowling) record.

Bragging Rights

Bravo, Melissa Horvat of Burlington, Ontario! You hold the female world record for the **Fastest Time to Score a Hat Trick**. On March 4, 2006, Horvat, who plays for the Burlington Barracudas Bantam 1 team, scored three consecutive goals in a mere 35 seconds.

Walking Stick

Someone get the sport of lacrosse a cane and some oatmeal, because it's the **Oldest Sport in Canada**.

Named after the Ojibwa word for "ball," the sport—originally called baggataway by Native Canadians—is a test of strength. While many claim that the sport was invented in 1683, early First Nations groups in Canada would play baggataway or lacrosse as a way of settling disagreements or training young, inexperienced warriors for battle. Because of its long-standing tradition in our country, lacrosse is Canada's official national sport. Sorry hockey.

Centenarian Shark

When you hear the words "stroke" and "senior" used in the same sentence, you tend to worry. But when that senior is Jaring Timmerman of Winnipeg, Manitoba, and that stroke is the backstroke, then it's cause for celebration. At the age of 100, Timmerman became the **Oldest Swimmer to Break Four World Records**.

During the Canadian Masters Swimming Championship held in Toronto in May 2009, Timmerman swam the 100-metre backstroke, in the age 100 to 104 category, in 3:51. The previously held record for that age category was 4:42. A month earlier, at the Manitoba Masters, Timmerman broke three other swimming world records in the same age category: one each in the 50-metre and 100-metre freestyle, and one more in the 50-metre backstroke.

Physically active his whole life, Timmerman did not start competing in the pool until he was 80 years old.

Long Feat

On September 10, 1892, Barnet Quina of Ottawa, Ontario, threw a lacrosse ball 148.91 metres—the **World's Longest Recorded Lacrosse Throw.**

Thermal Down Underwear

It is no surprise that Canucks would be able to walk 1300 kilometres through the bitter, harsh cold in order to reach the South Pole. What is surprising, however, is how fast they accomplished that frigid feat. On January 7, 2009, ultramarathon runner Ray Zab from Montréal, Québec, and his friends Montréaler Kevin Vallely and Edmonton Arctic-adventurer Richard Weber, reached the South Pole after a trek of just 33 days, 23 hours and 30 minutes—the **World's Fastest Trip Across Antarctica to the South Pole**. With no motorized vehicles to aid them on their journey, the triumphant trio employed cross-country skis, snowshoes and their very own feet in order to make it across Antarctica's Hercules Inlet and finally reach the bottom of the world. Thankfully, they did not fall off.

What the Puck!

Goaltender Terry Sawchuk from Winnipeg, Manitoba, holds the record for the **Most NHL Career Shutouts**—103.

World-Record Road Trip

Can you imagine how many times you would have to stop for bathroom breaks while traversing the Western Hemisphere by car?

Well, if you want to know, just ask Gary Sowerby of Moncton, New Brunswick, who along with American Tim Cahill set the **World Record for Speed in Driving the Entire Length of the American Continents**. In 1997, the two adventurers embarked on the mother of all road trips. Starting down in Argentina, the pair travelled north along the Pan-American Highway, reaching Alaska in their pickup truck 23 days, 22 hours and 43 minutes later.

Now recognized as a multi-world record holder in long-distance driving, Gary is colourfully known around the world as the "Indiana Jones of adventure driving."

Nimble Feat

In August 2008, a total of 623 fitness junkies gathered inside the Toronto Convention Centre, where Moira Merrithew, co-founder of Stott Pilates, led them in the **World's Largest Pilates Class**.

Guppy Love

If Vancouver, British Columbia's Elaine Tanner, a.k.a. Mighty Mouse for her small stature, didn't have lungs, you'd swear she was a fish.

One of this country's most decorated swimmers, Tanner was also the **Youngest Person to Receive the Lou Marsh Trophy**, which is given annually to Canada's best athlete, amateur or professional. In 1966, at the age of 15, Tanner was recognized as **Canada's Top Athlete of the Year**, after she became the first woman to win four gold medals and three silver medals at the Commonwealth Games that year.

Tanner followed up that victory with two more gold medals at the 1967 Pan American Games in Winnipeg.

But Tanner's biggest swimming achievement came during the 1968 Olympics Games in Mexico City, when she became the first person ever to win three medals—two silver and one bronze—in a single Olympics. I just hope that she never swims with all her medals around her neck, because she'd sink right to the bottom of the pool.

Backslash

It's hard enough to perform any task backwards, let alone in record time and underwater, but 20-year-old swimmer Lauren Lavigna from Vancouver, British Columbia, can do all three simultaneously.

In July 2009, at the World Aquatic Championships in Rome, Italy, Lavigna set a new record for the **World's Fastest Women's 200-metre Backstroke**. With a time of 2:10.03, Lavigna surpassed the previously held time of 2:11.16, which was set by fellow Canadian Jennifer Fratesi at the 2001 World Championships.

Bragging Rights

Yippee! In March 2009, Edmonton, Alberta's Annamay Pierse set the **World Record for Women's Short Course 200-Metre Breaststroke**, with a time of 2:17.50. She sunk the previous record of 2:17.75 like it was the *Titanic*, making her the King of the World!?

Feet of Fury

Cyclist Cornel Dobrin must have bionic legs of some sort, seeing as he holds the record for **Bicycling Across Canada in the Shortest Time**.

On July 1, 2009, the 24-year-old from Langley, British Columbia, left English Bay in Vancouver on his bicycle. After travelling for 24 days, Dobrin reached St. John's, Newfoundland, three days faster than the previous record of 27 days.

Managing to cover about 290 kilometres per day, Dobrin rode his bike 7200 kilometres in total. As for why he decided to take on the challenge, Dorbin has stated that curiosity was his main reason. So, it appears that curiosity may not only kill the cat, but it also inspires Canadians to bike across the country and set world records.

Keeping Up with the Joneses

If you hope to keep up with Canada's Neil Jones, you had better not be afraid of heights. In October 2008, Jones, along with England's Holly Budge and New Zealand's Wendy Smith, set two separate world records in one astounding leap of faith.

The first record was achieved when the trio jumped from Mount Everest, setting the **World Record for Skydiving from the Highest Peak**. On touchdown, the three set yet another record for **Landing on the World's Highest Drop Zone**, 3764 metres above the ground.

The Big Tow

After spending more than two days in the water, most people would look like living prunes. Fortunately for Ralph Hildebrand and Dave Phillips, they spent most of their two days on top of the water. On June 12, 1994, on Indian Arm, British Columbia, Hildebrand and Phillips set the record for the **World's Longest Water-Skiing Marathon**. Covering over 2152 kilometres while being towed behind a boat, the pair carved up the water for 56 hours and 35 minutes. To avoid collisions during the nighttime hours of their attempt, the pair used spotlights and infrared binoculars.

Asphalt All-Stars

If it weren't for cars, street hockey games would never have to end. The **World's Longest Street Hockey Game** actually took place in Lethbridge, Alberta.

The ball was dropped on August 20, 2008, and didn't stop moving until August 24. In total, the Lethbridge team ran, passed and scored for 105 hours and 17 minutes. For the record, the Lethbridge teams squashed the previous record set by a Winnipeg team in 2007 by more than five hours. Rumour has it that the Lethbridge team wanted to keep playing, but, unfortunately, their parents called them home for dinner.

What the Puck!

Wayne Gretzky has the **Most NHL Career Points—2857**. The Great One also holds the record for the **Most Goals in an NHL Career—894** in 20 seasons—as well as the record for the **Most Assists in an NHL Career—963** in 20 seasons.

The Human Propeller

Cyclist and entrepreneur Greg Kolodziejzyk of Calgary, Alberta, has a bright future at the stern of a boat—propelling it through the water. The titleholder of the **World's Farthest Distance Pedalled in a Human-Powered Boat in 24 Hours**, Kolodziejzyk pedalled 245.16 kilometres around a rectangular course on Montana's Whitefish Lake for a full day. Needless to say, after the repetitive feat was accomplished, it took Kolodziejzyk's legs another 24 hours to actually stop pedalling.

Leader of the Track

Q: Who's the **Greatest Canadian Race Driver** ever?

A: C'est Gilles Villeneuve.

Or, as his name is pronounced in English, Gilles Villeneuve.

Born in Richelieu, Québec, in 1950, Villeneuve won six Grand Prix races before meeting a tragic end in a 1982 crash during the Belgium Grand Prix. So, next time you see a car doing 200 kilometres per hour down a city street, shed a tear for the greatest racecar driver in Canadian history—then call the cops.

Attack of the Flying Snowmobiles

Why does Santa Claus need reindeer, when he could just as easily get Ross Mercer to teach him how to get his sleigh to fly all by itself?

On March 11, 2007, Mercer, who is from Whitehorse, Yukon, jumped his snowmobile into the record books with a distance of 80.3 metres. Mercer sailed over the previously held record of 74.6 metres and snagged the record for the **World's Longest Snowmobile Jump**.

Eye of the Tiger Shark

It takes a world-class athlete to break world records, which explains why Benoît Huot of Montréal, Québec, holds the world record for **Men's 100-Metre Butterfly**. Born with clubfeet, Huot trained to be a paralympic swimming champion. In 2000, he broke the previous record of 59.65 seconds in the 100-metre butterfly with a time of 59.54 seconds. Years later, at the 2004 Paralympic Games in Athens, Greece, Huot swam his way to five gold medals and three more world records.

Multi-Multi-Tasking

Jogging is very similar to being chased, except there isn't a knife-wielding maniac after you. However, to compensate for the missing element of danger, Michael Kapral of Toronto, Ontario, decided to toss juggling into the mix. Not only did he create an entirely new activity, known as the joggling, but Kapral began setting records in the new-fangled sport, including the **World's Fastest Marathon While Juggling Three Objects**.

After months of intensive training, Kapral was finally ready to attempt to break the record of two hours, 52 minutes, 15 seconds—set by an American joggler at the Philadelphia Marathon in 2006—and reclaim his title. Armed with three beanbags, Kapral entered the 2007 Scotiabank Toronto Waterfront Marathon, where his quest for Guinness World Record gold was achieved two hours, 50 minutes and nine seconds later. As a further display of his multi-tasking talent, Kapral not only juggled the entire length of the marathon, but he also chewed gum at the same.

The father of two, Kapral also holds the record for the **World's Fastest Marathon While Pushing a Baby in a Stroller**—two hours, 49 minutes. No word yet on whether or not Kapral will combine the two activities and try jogging while juggling babies.

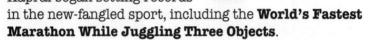

De-feat

Canada holds the record for the **Fewest Runs in a Cricket Game**. On February 19, 2003, the Canadian team managed just 36 runs, losing to Sri Lanka by nine wickets. Most cricket games have scores in the hundreds.

Out of Sight

Just because Valérie Grand'Maison of Montréal, Québec, was unable to see the finish line—she has a visual impairment—it didn't mean that she couldn't cross it in record time. In July 2008, at the Can-Am Open Championships for swimmers with a disability at Saanich Commonwealth Place in Victoria, British Columbia, the 19-year-old set the world record for **Disabled Women's 50-metre Backstroke**. Grand'Maison's time of 33.74 broke the previous record of 34.17 seconds.

What the Puck!

Colorado Avalanche Joe Sakic from Burnaby, British Columbia, has scored the **Most Overtime Game-Winning Goals**—seven.

A Leg Up on the Competition

From Terry Fox to Steve Fonyo and now to Orillia, Ontario's Rick Ball, Canada has a rich history of amputee runners who embody the determination it takes to become a true champion.

On May 23, 2009, Ball, who was outfitted with a carbon-fibre prosthetic leg, set the world record for the **Single-Leg Amputee 10-Kilometre Race**. With an inspiring time of 37 minutes and 55 seconds, Ball stepped all over the previous record of 38 minutes.

In April of the same year, Ball ran the Boston Marathon, where he set another record for an amputee runner competing in the able-bodied category. In total, it took Ball three hours, one minute and 50 seconds to run the

42-kilometre distance, besting the previous record by more than three minutes.

Batter Up and Up and Up and Up

Have you ever wished that a base-ball game would never end? Well, 40 players from Charlottetown, Prince Edward Island, came pretty close as they pitched, hit and bunted their way into the record books with the **World's Longest Softball Game**.

Players took to the field on July 8, 2008, and played ball for 96 hours and four minutes, beating the previous record of 95 hours and 23 minutes, set in Québec in July 2005. According to the rules, 20 players had to be involved in the game at all times. None of participants were allowed to leave the field unless injured, and everyone got a 30-minute break every six hours. The final score was Mark's Work Wearhouse 1066 runs, Hunter's Ale House 874 runs. Besides setting a new world record, the event also raised $10,000 for the Canadian Cancer Society.

The Golden Boy

Although his record has since been broken, speed skater Gaétan Boucher from Charlesbourg, Québec, once had the **Greatest Performance by a Canadian in the Olympic Games**. At the 1984 Games in Sarajevo, Boucher won two gold medals and one bronze—the most any Canadian athlete had ever won at an Olympics. For his outstanding performance, Boucher was awarded the Lou Marsh Trophy for Outstanding Male Athlete of the Year in 1984. Although his record stood for 22 years, it was finally shattered by Winnipeg speed skater Cindy Klassen at the 2006 Winter Games in Torino, where she won one gold, two silver and two bronze medals.

What the Puck!

The Edmonton Oilers scored the **Most Goals in an NHL Season**—446 in the 1983–84 season.

Stanley's Manly Award

Nowadays it's extremely rare to see a Canadian team hoist it above their heads, but the Stanley Cup, the **Oldest Sports Trophy in North America**, was originally Canadian. Donated in 1892 by the then–Governor General of Canada, Lord Frederick Stanley of Preston, the Cup was awarded annually to the top amateur hockey club in Canada. While many traditions surround the Cup, the most recognizable was started in 1950 by Detroit Red Wings team captain Ted Lindsay, who hoisted it above his head and skated around the rink in victory.

Rock Feat

From March 9 to 10, 2007, the Wheat City Curling Club in Brandon, Manitoba, played the **World's Longest Game of Curling**. Over the two-day period, the team of 10 curlers swept the ice for 40 hours and 23 minutes.

The _____est Athletes

Sweeping Souvenirs

Q: Who's got more rocks than a quarry?

A: The Turner Curling Museum, that's who.

Located in Weyburn, Saskatchewan, the facility houses the **World's Largest Collection of Curling Equipment** and features over 18,000 curling pins. The colossal curling collection began in the home of Don and Elva Turner. However, over time the collection grew, requiring more room. So, in 1990, the Turners relocated their museum to the local leisure centre. If you've never seen the Turner Curling Museum, then you had better hurry there—hurry hard.

Frostbite Me

Just because Canada is covered in ice and snow 10 months of the year, that doesn't mean we can't appreciate all that winter has to offer, like frostbite, especially when hockey is involved. November 22, 2003, saw 57,167 bundled-up fans attend the Heritage Classic, an outdoor hockey game between the Montréal Canadiens and the Edmonton Oilers that was held at Commonwealth Stadium in Edmonton, Alberta.

The mercury that day dipped down to −33°C with the wind chill, but it didn't stop faithful fans from setting the Canadian record for the **Largest Crowd to Attend a Hockey Game**. By the way, the final score of the game was 4-3 for Montréal.

What the Puck!

Sherwood Park, Alberta, holds the record for the **World's Longest Ice Hockey Game**—241 hours.

Aye, Aye, Skipper

Although she's never helmed a sailing vessel over the seven seas, Colleen P. Jones of Halifax, Nova Scotia, has steered her curling crew to a number of victories on the ice. Beginning her curling career at the age of 14, Jones is considered to be the **Most Successful Canadian Women's Skip in Curling History**. In 1982, at the age of 23, she also became the **Youngest Female to Win the Canadian Ladies' Championship**.

His Royal Highness

Nicknamed the "Prince of the Air," New Brunswick's Jay Cochrane is wired to set world records.

In 1972, Cochrane set the record for the **World's Farthest Distance on a Wire**. Suspended 36.5 metres above down-town Toronto, Cochrane inched his way 41 times across a 91-metre-long wire strung up between the Hockey Hall of Fame and the Canadian National Grandstand at the Canadian National Exposition. In total, Cochrane walked four kilometres in four hours and 34 minutes.

In 1981, he also broke the world record for the **Most Time Spent on a Wire**—21 days suspended above San Juan, Puerto Rico. Almost 10 years later, in 1995, Cochrane set the record for the **World's Longest and Highest Combined Skywalk**. In the span of 53 minutes, Cochrane walked 640 metres from one cliff edge to another, 408 metres above China's Yangtze River.

The following year, Cochrane was back up in the air and set a new record for the **World's Longest and Highest Nighttime Building-to-Building Skywalk**, walking 183 metres at a height of 160 metres.

But Cochrane's world records don't stop there. In 1998, he performed the **World's Longest and Highest Blind-folded Skywalk**, walking 183 metres at a height of 91 metres. The attempt secured Cochrane his fifth world record. Not one to rest on his laurels, in 2001, Cochrane set his sixth world record with the **World's Longest Building-to-Building Skywalk**. Balancing 667.5 metres in the air, it took Cochrane one hour and nine minutes to walk between two 40-storey buildings in Taiwan.

What the Puck!

Paul Stastny of Québec City, Québec, holds the NHL record for the **Longest Scoring Streak by a Rookie**—11 goals and 18 assists in 20 consecutive games.

Pitch Man

In 1957, while on the St. Louis Cardinals team, Glen Gorbous of Drumheller, Alberta, broke the record for the **World's Longest Baseball Throw**. Leaving his hand at 193 kilometres per hour, the ball soared a distance of 135.9 metres. And although no one ever wanted to play catch with Gorbous after that uncanny throw, his record still stands unbroken.

The Puck Stops Here!

Meet Martin Brodeur, a puckstopping-butterflyspreading-
five-holefearing-NHL-recordholding-goaltender for the
New Jersey Devils. Born in Montréal, Québec, Brodeur
has more NHL records than most goalies have teeth,
including the following:

☞ **Most Consecutive Seasons Winning 40 Games:**
6 seasons

☞ **Most Consecutive Seasons Winning 35 Games:**
10 seasons

☞ **Most Consecutive Seasons Winning 30 Games:**
11 seasons

☞ **Most Consecutive Team Wins to Start a Season:**
38 wins

☞ **Most Wins in a Season by a Goalie:** 48 wins

☞ **Most Minutes Played in an NHL Season:**
4434 minutes

☞ **Youngest Goalie to Win 400 NHL Games:** 31 years,
322 days

☞ **Youngest Goaltender to Win 300 NHL Games:**
29 years and 243 days

Tender feat

With 551 game wins under
his chest protector, Patrick
Roy of Sainte-Foy, Québec,
is considered the **Greatest
NHL Goaltender.**

Fore + Fore + Fore

On October 1, 2004, Sylvain Menard of Montréal, Québec, drove 7350 golf balls a distance of over 100 yards into a target area, giving him the record for the **Most Golf Balls Hit in 12 Hours**.

The Crosby Show

If age didn't matter, Sidney Crosby of Cole Harbour, Nova Scotia, would only have about half as many records as he does—which is still more than most people have. By the age of 19, Crosby was the captain of the Pittsburgh Penguins and had already amassed a number of NHL records, including:

☞ **Youngest Team Captain in the NHL**, at the age of 19 years, 297 days

☞ **Youngest Team Captain to Win the Stanley Cup** (in 2009)

☞ **First and Youngest Rookie to score 100 Points in an NHL Season**, at the age of 18 years, 253 days

☞ **Youngest Player to Score 200 Points in an NHL Season**, at the age of 19 years, 207 days

☞ **Youngest Person to Start in an NHL All-Star Game**, at the age of 19 years, 170 days

☞ Crosby also scored the game-winning goal in overtime at the 2010 Winter Olympics to give the Canadian men's hockey team the gold medal.

Touch and Gold

Chloe Hegland of Victoria, British Columbia, has a sense of touch that is so precise it has secured her two world records.

On December 12, 2006, the 10-year-old completed 155 touches (keeping a soccer ball in the air with your toes)—the **Most Touches Ever Performed in 30 seconds**. At the time, her record shattered both previous male and female records. Two years later, Hegland broke her own record with 163 touches in 30 seconds. To prove that she was more than a 30-seconder, on November 3, 2007, Hegland performed 339 touches in one minute— the best touch time of any female, ever.

What the Puck!

Cornwall, Ontario's Edouard "Newsy" Lalonde scored the **Most Consecutive Winning Goals in NHL History**—five.

He Is Ironman

Although Montréal, Québec's Peter Reid is not an iron-plated superhero, he does have the physique and stamina to be one.

In 2000, he received the (then) **Fastest Time for the Ironman World Championship (Hawaii)**, completing the race in a time of 8:21:01. Reid has won the event three times in his career. He also won 10 Ironman Triathlons before retiring in 2006.

Oh, Chute!

Parachutists fear absolutely nothing, except for the fear of forgetting to pack their parachutes. Luckily, Jason Moledzki of Toronto, Ontario, always remembers to wear his parachute, which may explain why he holds the record for the **World's Highest Speed Canopy Piloting**.

Canopy piloting is a recreational sport that involves a parachutist releasing the chute (canopy) at approximately 1524 metres above the earth. The parachutist then enters into a rotating dive to increase speed before beginning an obstacle course in the sky. On August 25, 2006, Moledzki completed one of these piloting courses in a record-breaking 2.72 seconds.

Light on your feat

Founded in 1939, the Royal Winnipeg Ballet holds tutu Canadian records—the **Oldest Dance Company in Canada** and the **Longest Continuously Operating Ballet Company in Canada**. For the record, it is also the second-oldest dance company in North America.

Ain't No Mountain High Enough

There ain't no Canadian mountain high enough for Calgary, Alberta, mountaineer Jack Bennett, because he has climbed them all. Bennett holds the record for the **Most Canadian High Points Climbed**. It may have taken him five years and 361 days to climb the highest peak in each of the 10 provinces and three territories, but on June 15, 1998, Bennett reached the final summit. As for why Bennett climbed to the apex of all those mountains, one can only assume that he really loves to yodel.

60-Minute Workout

In the business world of push-ups, Roy Berger of Ottawa, Ontario, would be a rep-ceptionist because of all the push-ups he does.

Berger's bulging biceps have not only earned him the title of Mr. Push-Up, they have landed him in the record books for the **Most Push-ups in One Hour**. On August 30, 1998, Mr. Push-up pushed his way up and down and up and down again 3416 times in one hour. In February 2004, Berger was back it at, completing 138 push-ups in one minute.

Welcome to the Gun Show

Don Pruden must have the biggest guns (arms) in the country, because he has broken more push-up world records than anyone else in Canada—sorry, Mr. Push-up. In 2003, Pruden performed the **Most One-Armed Push-ups in 30 minutes**—1382. He then performed the **Most One-Armed Push-ups in 10 Minutes**—546. Then in 2005, just for kicks, he performed the **Most One-armed Back-of-Hand Push-ups in One Hour**—677. Pruden holds many other records as well, which are mostly variations of his previous push-up feats, including:

- ☞ 5557 fist push-ups in three hours
- ☞ 1781 back-of-hand push-ups in one hour
- ☞ 1382 one-arm push-ups in 30 minutes
- ☞ 1045 back-of-hand push-ups in 30 minutes
- ☞ 1000 fist push-ups in 18 minutes
- ☞ 575 back-of-hand push-ups in 15 minutes
- ☞ 546 one-arm push-ups in 10 minutes
- ☞ 114 one-arm push-ups in one minute

Don't Mock the Boat

Don't bother bringing your 100-metre-long boat to the **World's Longest Canoe Race**, because it's not a race for super-long canoes at all, but a long-distance canoe race. On May 24, 1967, the Canadian Government Centennial Voyageur Canoe Pageant and Race departed down the North Saskatchewan River from Rocky Mountain House, Alberta. Contestants reached Montréal, Québec, on September 4, just in time for Expo '67. In total, canoeists paddled 5283 kilometres along the same route that early Canadian voyageurs would have travelled to get from Alberta to Québec.

Ice Queen

So fast she melted the ice, after back-to-back gold medal wins at the 1998 and 2002 Winter Olympic Games, Saskatoon, Saskatchewan, speed skater Catriona LeMay Doan was unofficially dubbed the **Fastest Woman on Ice**.

Bragging Rights

Yippee! Oakville, Ontario's Adam van Koeverden holds the record for the **World's Fastest Canoe/ Kayak 500-Metre Flatwater K1 (Male)**, which he set on August 19, 2008, at the Beijing Olympics with a time of 1:35.554. We canoe you could do it, Adam!

See Tom Run

Do you ever wonder if the friends of long-distance runners sometimes bet them that they can't run a certain distance, just so they can get rid of them for a while?

Well, you can be sure that the friends of Tom Longboat never did anything like that to him.

Born in 1887 on the Six Nations of the Grand River Reserve near Brantford, Ontario, Longboat is **Canada's Best Long-Distance Runner**. In 1907, he won the Boston Marathon in record time, and he was so quick on his feet that he was made a dispatch runner during World War I. Unfortunately, he was mistakenly declared dead during the war, prompting his wife to remarry.

Every year in Toronto, Longboat is honoured at the Toronto Island Run. However, Tom longboat's coolest legacy is that he once raced a horse and won.

Gutter Feat

Toronto, Ontario's Andy Milne gave a whole new meaning to "sleeping in the gutter" after he bowled for 120 hours straight—the **World's Longest Bowling Marathon**.

Lady in the Lake

Or should it be "Lady in the Channel"? Either way, that's where you would find Toronto, Ontario's Marilyn Bell, if you were looking for her. On September 9, 1954, at the age of 16, Bell became the **First Person to Swim Across Lake Ontario**, a distance of 52 kilometres. She completed the distance in 20 hours and 59 minutes. On July 31, 1955, she became the **Youngest Person to Swim the English Channel**.

Bell was inducted into Canada's Sports Hall of Fame in 1958, and, in 1993, she entered the Canadian Swimming Hall of Fame and was named one of the top Canadian athletes of the century.

What the Puck!

The Calgary Flames had the **Most Consecutive NHL Games Scoring a Goal**—at least one goal every game for a total of 264 goals scored between November 1981 and January 1985.

Fastest Feet in the North

It must have been difficult to take a school photo of Oakville, Ontario's Donovan Bailey, since he would eventually go on to become **Canada's Fastest Man**. At one point, he was also the **World's Fastest Man**.

At the 1996 Atlanta Olympic Games, Bailey did his country proud when he sprinted 100-metres in 9.84 seconds, winning the gold medal and the title of fastest human alive. In 1997, Bailey defended his title against American sprinter Michael Johnson at a race in Toronto's SkyDome. Needless to say, Bailey ripped it up again.

Canada's Other Fastest Man

Canada has a track record of producing world-class sprinters, and Percy Williams of Vancouver, British Columbia, was one of our first. At the age of 20, Williams won gold medals in both the 100-metre and 200-metre sprints at the 1928 Amsterdam Olympic Games.

To Sire with Love

When a horse wins the coveted Kentucky Derby, it becomes the **World's Leading Sire**. Called the most successful and influential sire in thoroughbred history, Canada's Northern Dancer was a world-renowned race-horse. So much so, that Toronto named a street after him, Woodbine Race Track erected a bronze statue of him, and Canada Post gave him his own postage stamp, which should be for mail sent via the Pony Express.

Track Record

If you've been to every Queen's Plate horse race, then you've spent way too much time at the track. Established in June 1860 and held annually at the Carleton Track in Toronto, Ontario, the Queen's Plate is now the **Oldest Horse Race in North America**. The first horse to win the event was a mare named Don Juan. All the horses that enter the annual race must be three years of age and bred in Canada—talk about a one-shot deal. Horses are permitted to run in the Queen's Plate only once, so no horsing around.

What the Puck!

Chris Simon of Wawa, Ontario, received the **Most Severe Suspension in the NHL**—25 games—for attacking a New York Rangers player with his stick.

Power Ball

He may not want to brag about it—for fear of being burglarized—but Calgary, Alberta-born comic book artist Todd McFarlane owns the **World's Most Valuable Baseball**. On January 12, 1999, the man who created the comic book character Spawn purchased Mark McGuire's 70th homerun ball for $3,054,000.

Holy Sheets!

In 1909, the Regina Curling Club erected what was then the **World's Biggest Curling Rink**. Located in downtown Regina, Saskatchewan, the facility featured an unheard of nine sheets of ice. An innovator in the sport, the Regina

Curling Club formed in 1889, with only eight pairs of curling rocks to its name. Three years later, the club organized the first-ever bonspiel in the Northwest Territories (of which Saskatchewan was then still part).

Freight Train

Known as the "Big Train," Lionel Conacher of Toronto, Ontario, who lived from 1900 to 1954, is considered to be the **Greatest All-Round Canadian Athlete**. Before he was 18 years old, Conacher won the Ontario wrestling title and the Canadian light heavyweight boxing title. He also excelled at hockey, football, lacrosse, baseball and, yes, politics, as a Liberal MP. In 1950, Lionel Conacher was selected as **Canada's Male Athlete of the Half-Century**.

Bragging Rights

Shake that half-century fanny of yours, Fanny "Bobbie" Rosenfeld! You're the *Greatest Canadian Female Athlete of the Half-Century*. Born in 1905, in Barrie, Ontario, Bobbie played baseball, basketball, hockey, tennis and also ran track. In 1928, she set distance records in the long jump, standing broad jump and discus. All of Rosenfeld's records held until the 1950s.

Whatever Floats Your Boat

Whatever floats the Royal St. John's Rowing Regatta's boat has been doing it for over three centuries. **North America's Oldest Continuous Sporting Event**, the regatta is held on Newfoundland's Quidi Vidi Lake on the first Wednesday of every August. The earliest recorded race took place in 1816; however, many believe that the competition was held as early as the 1700s. The massive event, which attracts more the 50,000 spectators, is so popular that Regatta Day is a civic holiday in St. John's, Newfoundland.

Quarterback with Cheese

Q: Where did the **Greatest Canadian-born Quarterback** live?

A: In a "hut hut."

Just kidding, Russ Jackson actually lived in Ottawa, Ontario, where he was QB number one for the Ottawa Rough Riders for 12 years. Jackson led his team to three Grey Cup victories and was ranked eighth in the list of Top 50 CFL Players of All Time. He is also the highest ranked Canadian-born player on that list, so that makes him extra great.

cleat feat

Founded in 1910, the Saskatchewan Roughriders are the **Oldest Continuously Operating Football Club in Western Canada**.

Canada's Got Sole

Way to walk, Canada. You hold the record for the **World's Largest Number of People Walking One Kilometre at the Same Time**.

On October 3, 2007, 231,635 Canadians simultaneously stepped one kilometre at over 1000 different venues throughout the country. That number of Canadian participants walked all over the previously held record of 100,915 walkers, set in Australia in 2006.

It's All Downhill

During the 1976 Olympics in Innsbruck, Austria, 18-year-old Kathy Kreiner Phillips from Timmins, Ontario, became the **Youngest Gold Medallist in Alpine Skiing**.

Canuck à la CART

If you're ever late for work or school, get Scarborough, Ontario's Paul Tracy to drive you. This Champ Car World Series racecar driver holds the record for the **Most CART (Championship Auto Racing Teams) Race Wins**—26.

The 2010 Winter olympics

And One More Makes...

Canadian athletes gave hip-hop artists a run for their money with all the bling they were sporting at the Vancouver 2010 Winter Olympic Games. Hours before the games ended on February 28, 2010, the Canadian Men's hockey team clinched their country's 14th gold medal of the Games. With that newly minted medal secured, Canada broke the previous record held by Norway for the **Most Gold Medals at a Single Winter Games**.

Female Speed Feat

Cindy Klassen of Winnipeg, Manitoba, is the current holder of the world record for the **Fastest Speed Skater, Long Track**. On March 25, 2006, Klassen skated the 1000-metre track in one minute, 13 seconds—a speed of nearly 50 kilometres per hour! She also holds the world record for the 1500-metre and 3000-metre distances.

The _____est Athletes

She Shoots, She Scores…and Scores…and Scores…

On February 17, 2010, Hayley Wickenheiser of Shaunavon, Saskatchewan, stickhandled her way into the record books during a 13–1 win over the Swedish women's hockey team, when the Canadian women's hockey team captain scored her 16th Olympic career goal—the **Most Goals Scored in the Winter Olympic Games**.

Three Times the Lady

While some women choose to keep their hats in a box, Canadian women's hockey team member Meghan Agosta of Windsor, Ontario, keeps hers on the ice. On February 17, 2010, in a game against Sweden, the 23-year-old forward scored her third Olympic hat trick—the **Most Winter Olympic Hat Tricks**, ever.

What the Puck!

Paul Henderson of Kincardine, Ontario, scored the **Most Famous Goal in Canadian History** (at least until Sidney Crosby's 2010 Olympics golden goal). During the 1972 Summit Series against the Russians, with the score tied and 34 seconds left on the clock, Henderson nailed down the legendary win for Team Canada.

Boob Tubing

While watching Olympic events on television is not yet an Olympic event, it is now a record-setting one. On

February 28, 2010, 10.6 million Canadians tuned into the Olympic gold medal game to watch Canada's men's hockey team beat the U.S. team 3–2 in overtime. Even Canadian troops stationed in Kandahar had their eyes glued to the monumental matchup, which is now considered to be the **Most-Watched Sports Program in Canadian History**. Ten days earlier, on February 19, 2010, the Vancouver 2010 Winter Olympic Games opening ceremony garnered 13.3 million Canadian viewers, making it the **Most-watched Canadian Television Event in History**.

Male Speed Feat

Humboldt, Saskatchewan's Jeremy Wotherspoon once held the world record for the 1000-metre event in speed skating, with a time of one minute and eight seconds. He was also once considered to be the **World's Fastest Speed Skater, Long Track**. On November 9, 2007, Wotherspoon skated his way to a world record in the 500-metres, with a time of 34.03. Previously, he had picked up a silver medal in the 500-metres at the 1998 Nagano Olympic Games.

Eternal Flame

Since it is the second largest country in the world, it would make perfect sense that Canada would claim the mantle of the **World's Longest Olympic Torch Relay**. Commencing on October 30, 2009, in Victoria, British Columbia, and ending on February 12, 2010, at BC Place

The _____est Athletes

stadium in Vancouver, British Columbia (106 days), the Vancouver 2010 Winter Olympic Games torch travelled approximately 45,000 kilometres—the **Most Kilometres Ever Travelled by an Olympic Torch Within the Borders of a Host Country**. On its trip crisscrossing our great land, it was carried by 12,000 different torchbearers.

Rubber Ski Boots

Athletes, trainers, coaches and ticket holders at the 2010 Vancouver Winter Olympic Games had to wear raincoats and sunscreen instead of tuques and parkas as the mercury hit record highs. On average, Winter Olympic host countries tend to have temperatures well below zero; Vancouver, however, doesn't fit that model. With daily temperatures well in excess of 10°C, the 2010 games became the **Warmest Winter Olympic Games** in history. Many of the downhill-skiing events had to be rescheduled because of poor snow conditions.

Population Boom

When Canada throws a party, the whole world attends, which is why we now hold the world record for the **Most Competitors at a Winter Olympic Games**. In total, 82 countries participated in the 2010 Vancouver Winter Olympics. That's two countries more than the previous record held by the 2006 Turin Winter Olympic Games.

The Golden Girls

While they may not be completely covered in solid gold just yet, Canada's women's hockey team is certainly well decorated with the precious metal. On February 25, 2010, at the 2010 Vancouver Winter Olympic Games, the Canadian women's team scored their third Olympic gold medal win, the **Most Winter Olympic Hockey Gold Medals for a Women's Team**.

Mental Workout

1. Who is the longest-serving team captain in NHL history?
    A. Ray Bourque
    B. Steve Yzerman
    C. Sidney Crosby
    D. Captain Crunch

2. Who played the most games in his NHL career?
    A. Mark Messier
    B. Chris Chelios
    C. Gordie Howe
    D. Muhammad Ali

3. In which NHL game did the teams score the most goals in a single game?
    A. Montréal Canadiens vs. Toronto St. Patricks
    B. Montréal Canadiens vs. Québec Bulldogs
    C. Montréal Canadiens vs. Winnipeg Jets
    D. Montréal Canadiens vs. California Golden Seals

4. Which NHL team has won the most Stanley Cups?
    A. Toronto Maple Leafs
    B. Montréal Canadiens
    C. Detroit Red Wings
    D. Harlem Globetrotters

Answers on pages 240–41.

The _____ est Athletes

The Line of Scrubbage

The recreation centre's equipment manager has just quit, leaving a pile of sweaty, smelly sports equipment in the middle of the locker room floor. Now, as the centre's senior staff member, it is your job to hand wash each of the following pieces of athletic apparatus and return them to their proper activity.

Hockey	Finger tab
Badminton	Spikes
Football	Spray skirt
Soccer	Leotard
Lacrosse	Goggles
Baseball	Seat belt
Tennis	Tee
Skiing	Pin
Golf	Shuttlecock
Archery	Neck guard
Auto racing	Neck roll
Bowling	Shin guards
Gymnastics	Crosse
Kayaking	Base
Running	Sweatbands

Answers on page 241.

Word Game Misconduct

A word brawl has broken out on the field, and both benches have been cleared. Now, as the team's mascot, it is your job to go out there and untangle the two teams of sports terms before halftime is over.

UMRONEH _____

BNUT _____

LAWK _____

KEIRTS _____

TOSOB _____

LIANEP _____

ILTZB _____

CKLOB _____

CEDKALFBI _____

ISGHSALN _____

EIOFDSF _____

CENFEOF _____

ACFILOFIS _____

AAENR _____

STSSAI _____

LSMEANNI _____

IRPEOD _____

LAPYER _____

IPONT _____

ERTHCAC _____

Answers on page 241.

The _____est Athletes

Lacrosse Word

You have been chosen as one of the team captains for the scrimmage Lacrosse game, but before you can pick your first teammate, you must use the clues provided below to fill in the blanks.

ACROSS

3. Edmonton's gridiron group
6. Time to tie break
7. Icy entertainment
10. A defensive act in football
12. Causing a misstep
13. Out of bounds
14. No rules
16. Baseball and bowling have this in common
18. Winnipeg punters

DOWN

1. Hockey disc
2. Goaltender and banking have this in common
4. Cat burglar and baseball player have this in common
5. Referee's tool
8. Follows "loading" or "twilight"
9. Grass substitute
11. Skiing and Thanksgiving act
15. The kings of British Columbia
17. Avian golf term

Answers on page 241.

Super Fan-Demonium

To cheer their team on, the roaring crowd wants to spell out sports expressions using letters that have been printed on oversized cards. Unfortunately, all the cards have been shuffled together, and the crowd can't figure them out. As the hotdog vendor, it is your job to sort through the letters and help the horde boost the team's morale and win the game.

```
S U S P E N S I O N F R T E N D C L M U T
C A N U C K S A M E U N R V N G G F F S D
E D E P A R D L P E M I B E E F L F N S E
G A M E G F E T E S B A J S N B O K I L F
P I T C O A B A U E L T E G S D V R M I E
C A N U A C O N S Y E P R C E J E I C N N
B T L N L K I U S E M A L F D E S E I E S
A C L U P F L O N J D C I F U R D L E M E
C E D E P M A T S E E N B U R L G D L E I
K A R P I T C H E R F U N M E S L N D N E
F D O F F S I D E S E O B B R S R B I K L
I F I S U S P N I E R S L O P E S F A C D
E U L P M A T U E Y O L T F A C A U I C I
L M E L M U T O L D T A F K N R L M E N K
D B R S U S P M D C N O D C U C D B L U R
R A S P M A T R H E L M U T O A F S D O C
S P E A R I N G S A D L I N E B A C K E R
```

Canucks	Crease	Icing	Linebacker
Flames	Defense	Jersey	Linemen
Oilers	Offside	Spearing	Slopes
Senators	Foul	Suspension	Mound
Boards	Enforce	Stampede	Pitcher
Net	Game	Backfield	
Goal	Gloves	Fullback	
Captain	Helmut	Fumble	

The _____est Athletes

The _____est Construction

Narrowest	Tallest
Smallest	Soundest
Oldest	Creakiest
Shakiest	Wackiest
Ugliest	Trashiest
Tiniest	Roomiest
Quaintest	Wobbliest
Cheapest	Sleekest

(Superlative recommendations for chapter title—pick one or add your own)

Civilized Engineering

If you didn't know much about Canada, then you would likely buy into the myth that the Great White North consists of nothing more than millions and millions of igloos. And while we are more than capable of constructing a 13-storey, dome-shaped ice palace complete with a swimming pool, central air conditioning and a walk-in refrigerator in under a week, Canadians prefer to construct other marvels of architecture and design.

Way back in 1670, when other countries were still burning witches at the stake, Canada established the world's first chain store, the Hudson's Bay Company. And the assembling of mega-structures didn't stop there. In the following years, the inhabitants of Québec City would fortify their city by erecting massive, record-setting protective walls to keep invading forces at bay. Meanwhile, on the Prairies, monstrous barns, huge basilicas and enormous churches were challenging structural standards.

As the years rolled on, Canada would delve even further into the development of projects that would dwarf other edifices around the world. A few of these record-breaking builds included a seemingly never-ending walking path, a single highway that would eventually connect every province and territory, a teetering tower in the middle of a downtown metropolis and hydroelectric power plants and dams that humble other similar constructions.

And when bigger became synonymous with better, Canada bucked the trend and built baby-sized structures,

The _____est Construction

like a microscope museum and a compact correctional facility. So the next time someone says that Canada is nothing but a bunch of igloos, tell them to feast their eyes on the _____est construction.

A Site for Small Eyes

Featuring a merman, psychic frogs and Satan's pitchfork, the **World's Smallest Museum** is the work of Gerri Ann Siwek and her husband, Steve Karch.

Based in Buena, Saskatchewan, and known throughout Canada as Funomena: the Weird and Strange Mobile Museum, the couple's eccentric collection is housed inside a mobile trailer that Ann and Steve drive around the countryside every summer. Funomena has even taken its weird and strange assortment of curiosities to the weirdest and strangest country in the world, the U.S., with stopovers in Texas, Michigan and Minnesota.

Construction Ahead

Slow down! You're approaching the Albert Memorial Bridge in Regina, Saskatchewan. Measuring approximately 56 metres long, 22 metres wide and spanning the narrowest point of Wascana Creek, which is 20 metres across, the Albert Memorial Bridge is the **Largest Bridge Over the Shortest Span of Water in the World**.

A Table for Boo

If you're in the mood for some culinary delights as well as frights, please make a reservation at Winnipeg's

Oldest Restaurant. Established on Portage Avenue in 1918, the Chocolate Shop is no longer the cavity-inducing sweetshop that its name implies, but a restaurant and culinary school specializing in traditional Aboriginal cuisine, including bannock and bison.

In addition to drawing patrons from around the world, the eatery also attracts otherworldly phantoms. Considered to be one of the most haunted sites in the city, the bistro regularly welcomes paranormal enthusiasts and ghost tours into the bowels of its creepy cellar, where strange sightings are a daily occurrence. An apparently permanent feature, located in the farthest corner of the dark and dreary basement, is a black stain that cannot be removed, no matter how often it is scrubbed. Rumour has it that the ominous black blot is actually a vortex into the spirit realm. So, if you ever visit the Chocolate Shop, don't forget to tip your ghostess.

Bragging Rights

You're so money, Montréal Exchange. Established in 1832, it was the first stock exchange in Canada and is now the **Oldest Exchange in Canada**.

Holy Moly!

OMG! The Holy Trinity Anglican Church near Stanley Mission, Saskatchewan, is the **Oldest Church in Western Canada**.

Built on the north bank of the Churchill River between 1854 and 1860, this grand cathedral is known for its gothic-inspired steeple and its 37 gothic-style windows, containing over 1000 pieces of stained glass, which were shipped over from England during the initial construction phase. Recognized as a Provincial Historic Site, the church is also the **Oldest Standing Building in Saskatchewan**. To this day, religious services are still held in the hurch every Sunday. However, because it is accessible only by boat, your Sunday best may get a little wet.

Creaky feat

Built in 1864, the Clerk's Quarters in Fort Victoria, located between Cold Lake and Edmonton, is the **Oldest Building in Alberta**. The fort was established by the Hudson's Bay Company as a trading post.

Take a Hike

Stock up on trail mix—this is going to be a very long walk. Stretching along the Niagara Escarpment for more than 880 kilometres, the Bruce Trail is **Canada's Oldest and Longest Footpath**.

Established in the 1960s, the route winds through the lush southern and central Ontario countryside, which is teeming with dense woods, wondrous waterfalls and raging rivers. You should bring a sleeping bag if you plan to complete the entire length of the footpath—in total, if you hiked the trail for eight hours per day, it would take you nearly a month to complete it end to end.

Construction Ahead

Slow down! You're approaching the Trans-Canada Highway—the **World's Longest National Highway**. Work on the super-highway began in Victoria, British Columbia, on April 25, 1950. It then moved eastward toward St. John's, Newfoundland and Labrador. Although the highway opened on September 3, 1962, it was not officially completed until 1971. The total cost of building the 7821-kilometre piece of paved roadway was in excess of $ 1 billion.

The Extreme Highway

If you ever find yourself on the Dempster Highway, you are probably really lost. Considered the **Northern-most Highway in Canada**, the Dempster Highway straddles the border between the Yukon and the Northwest Territories and is the only public road above the Arctic Circle that is open year-round.

Covering a distance of 720 kilometres, the highway, which opened in 1979, runs from Dawson, Yukon, to Inuvik, Northwest Territories, utilizing ice bridges and ferries along the way. Originally a dogsled trail, the expansion of oil production in the country's northern areas warranted the construction of an access road. Sitting upon a thick layer of gravel, the highway was specially designed to withstand the harsh winter climate and the thawing of the ground in spring.

Bragging Rights

The Superpower Plant

If the James Bay project had a superpower, it would be hydroelectricity. And if it had a secret identity, it would be...the **Largest Hydroelectric Power Development in Canada**.

Consisting of a number of hydroelectric power stations, eight dams and over 190 dikes containing five reservoirs, the project, located on Québec's La Grande River, covers 11,900 square kilometres—half the size of Lake Ontario. Construction of the massive power station began in the 1970s. But it was not until 1982, and billions of dollars later, that it finally opened. In total, the project's generating systems have a combined output of 16,000 megawatts—three times more than that of the Hoover Dam.

Dam Feat

At 242 metres above bedrock, the Mica Dam on the Columbia River 135 kilometres north of Revelstoke, British Columbia, is the **Highest Dam in Canada**.

Take a Bow

When you've been in the entertainment business as long as the Lyric Theatre, you get to pay the seniors' admission price. Constructed in 1912, this Swift Current landmark is **Saskatchewan's Oldest Operating Theatre**. Beginning as a stage for vaudeville performers, the venue was later converted into a movie theatre. Subsequent to that, it became a popular bar and nightclub. These days, however, the Lyric has returned to its roots, offering audiences live performances and weekly open-stage events.

Bragging Rights

Wunderbar, Kimberly, British Columbia! You're the **Highest City in Canada**. With an elevation of 1113 metres, Kimberly has embraced its altitude by adopting a Bavarian theme, which includes the **World's Largest Free-standing Cuckoo Clock**.

Open for Business

Without commerce, a hamlet cannot flourish. And without liquor, a hamlet couldn't celebrate its success. Fortunately, R.H. Corbett solved both problems by opening up what was to become the **Longest Running Business in Swift Current**. As a necessary step in obtaining a liquor licence, Corbett built the Imperial Hotel—or the Big "I" as it is commonly known—in 1903, to help Swift Current to gain village status, which it did on March 15, 1907.

The _____est Construction

Construction Ahead

Slow down! You're approaching the Hudson's Bay Company. Established in 1670, it is the **Oldest Company in Canada**, the **Oldest Commercial Corporation in North America** and one of the oldest companies in the world.

Stay Out!

If you are of British descent, you may have a hard time getting into Québec City. The **Oldest Walled City in North America**, Québec's Old Town was barricaded behind ramparts (protective walls) during the 1770s in order to protect the capital of New France from the invading British. Although France eventually relinquished control of Canada to the British, to this day, many of the original retaining walls still stand, protecting Québec from modern English-speaking invaders such as non-bilingual media outlets and cross-Canada promotional contests.

Construction Ahead

Slow down! You're approaching St. John's, Newfoundland. Discovered by explorer John Cabot on June 24, 1497, St. John's is the **Oldest City in North America**.

Snow Border

The easiest way for foreigners to sneak across the Canadian border is to pretend that they are hockey players. However, a disguise may not even be necessary because

Canada has the **World's Longest Undefended and Open Border**. For a combined total of 8893 kilometres along the southern Canada-U.S. border and the Canada-Alaska border, the "True North, Strong and Free" isn't just a saying, it's our philosophy.

Bragging Rights

A tip of the wing goes out to Toronto's Lester B. Pearson International Airport. In 2008, the airport welcomed 32.3 million travellers to its terminal, making it the **Largest and Busiest Airport in Canada**.

Barnzilla

If you're looking to host North America's largest barn dance, then you had better rent the **Largest Barn in North America**. At one time, that building could be found in southwestern Saskatchewan.

In the 1900s, a farmer from Kentucky named William "Horseshoe" Smith moved to Leader, Saskatchewan, to raise livestock. But with 2000 horses, 2000 hogs, 10,000 sheep and 1600 mules to his name, Smith quickly ran out of room. To solve the predicament, he decided to build a barn capable of housing his entire menagerie. In 1914, Smith and a crew of at least 100 men began construction of the barn, which would eventually measure 122 metres long, 39 metres wide and 18 metres high.

The _____est Construction

The barn took approximately five months to complete. Unfortunately, Smith died only a few years after it was erected. With no one left to maintain it, the behemoth barn was torn down. Today, only the foundation of the super-shed remains.

Genealogist in a Bottle

With over 20,000 books, articles, and other items available for Saskatchewan's citizens to trace their family trees, the Saskatchewan Genealogical Society Library is **Canada's Largest Genealogical Lending Library**. But just remember to return any and all borrowed items to the library on time, or else your family's lineage could end with you.

Moccasined Feat

With a diameter of 213 metres and a height of 33 metres, the Treaty Four Governance Centre in Fort Qu'Appelle, Saskatchewan, is the **World's Largest Inhabited Tipi**.

Cramped Quarters

Make sure that you and your friends walk single file down Victoria, British Columbia's Fan Tan Alley, or you could end up wedged in there forever. The **Narrowest Street in Canada**, the alley, which once housed opium dens and gambling establishments, is a mere 1.2 metres wide.

Construction Ahead

Slow down! You're approaching the Saint Boniface Basilica Cathedral. Constructed in the 1880s, the cathedral is the **Oldest Building in Winnipeg**. What's more, the body of Louis Riel—Métis leader, political agitator and folk hero—was laid to rest in the cathedral's graveyard, which is **Western Canada's Oldest Catholic Cemetery**.

What's the Skinny?

It's no surprise that the only people who work in Vancouver, British Columbia's Sam Kee Building are stick figures. Standing 30 metres long and 1.5 metres wide, it is the **Narrowest Commercial Building in Canada**.

Tall Feat

Topping out 201 metres above the street, the 62-storey Living Shangri-la skyscraper is the **Tallest Building in Vancouver**.

The _____est Construction

Don't Look Down!

Any troll looking to live under the Capilano Suspension Bridge better not be afraid of heights. Hovering a dizzying 70 metres above the Capilano River in North Vancouver, British Columbia, the Capilano Suspension Bridge is **Canada's Longest Suspension Footbridge**. The 136-metre-long structure was the brainchild of Scottish civil engineer George  Grant Mackay, who began construction of the bridge in 1888. The original structure was built out of cedar planks and hemp rope, but years later, it was refurbished with a stronger wire cable. Besides being a national treasure, the Capilano Suspension Bridge is also a tourist haven, attracting over 800,000 sightseers a year. A popular shooting destination for Hollywood productions, the bridge has welcomed scores of celebrities over the years, including Mick Jagger and Marilyn Monroe.

Construction Ahead

Slow down! You're approaching the famous stretch of railway that runs between Regina and Stoughton, Saskatchewan. Consisting of 140 kilometres of rail that does not bend, twist or curve, this is the **Longest Straight Line of Rail in the World**.

Old School

If someone tells you that they were a member of the University of New Brunswick's first graduating class, you are either talking to a liar or an immortal. Founded in Fredericton and St. John's, New Brunswick, in 1785, UNB is the **Oldest University in Canada**. What's more, it is tied with the University of Georgia in Atlanta as the **Oldest School in North America**.

Bragging Rights

Hey, Confederation Bridge—with 2000 cars crossing your span every hour, you're the **World's Longest Continuous Marine Span Bridge**. Straddling the 13-kilometre distance over the Northumberland Strait from Borden, PEI, to mainland New Brunswick, the Confederation Bridge cost over $1 billion to construct and opened on May 31, 1997.

Water Under a Covered Bridge

Constructed in 1897, New Brunswick's Hartland Bridge is the **World's Longest Covered Bridge**. Spanning 390-metres, the conduit was originally topless. But in 1921, after a faulty span was repaired, the bridge re-opened with a sturdy, new roof.

Construction Ahead

Slow down! You're approaching the Mount MacDonald Railway Tunnel, near Rogers Pass, BC—the **Longest Tunnel in the Americas**. Carved through Mount MacDonald, the tunnel stretches 14.7 kilometres.

Biblical Proportions

If you've got booze, just drive on through. Settled by Mormons in the late-1880s, Cardston, Alberta, is not only an alcohol-free town, it's also the home of the **Biggest Mormon Temple in Canada**. Spread out over four hectares of sacred land, this holy monument stands 26 metres tall and has a floor area of over 7590 square metres. It is also the **Oldest Latter Day Saints Church Outside the U.S**. The temple has been a National Historic Site since 1992.

Don't Mock the Boat

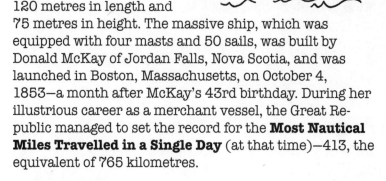

If you got seasick aboard the *Great Republic*, you'd have puked on a legend. Known as the **World's Largest Wooden Clipper Ship**, the *Great Republic* weighed about 6000 tonnes and measured approximately 120 metres in length and 75 metres in height. The massive ship, which was equipped with four masts and 50 sails, was built by Donald McKay of Jordan Falls, Nova Scotia, and was launched in Boston, Massachusetts, on October 4, 1853—a month after McKay's 43rd birthday. During her illustrious career as a merchant vessel, the Great Republic managed to set the record for the **Most Nautical Miles Travelled in a Single Day** (at that time)—413, the equivalent of 765 kilometres.

Shopping Mole

Don't forget to wear your designer miner's helmet when you shop Toronto's PATH Walkway. The **World's Largest Underground Shopping Centre**, PATH is an underground network that connects foot traffic to a subterranean shopping experience you'll not soon forget. Designed in the 1960s as a way of relieving the overcrowded sidewalks of Toronto, today PATH sprawls underground for 27 kilometres and encompasses five subway stations and over

1200 retail outlets. Unfortunately, the food court in this subsurface shopping mall offers nothing to eat besides carrots, beets, peanuts and potatoes.

Bragging Rights

You grow, girl! Established in 1848, the Byward Market in Ottawa, Ontario, is the **Oldest Continuously Operating Outdoor Market in Canada**.

Don't Trip

Mind your step when inside the Four Seasons Centre for the Performing Arts City Room in Toronto, Ontario. Spanning four storeys and 46 metres, the crystal-and-iron steps, which hang from the ceiling of the 2071-seat theatre, make up the **World's Longest Freespan Staircase**.

A Short Sentence

You didn't have to be a small-time criminal or have committed petty larceny to serve time in what is claimed to be the **World's Smallest Jail**—you just couldn't take up much room. Stationed in Tweed, Ontario, this petite penitentiary measures 4.8 metres by six metres and houses three iron-barred cells. In operation from 1899 to 1950, the small slammer now houses Tweed's tourist information booth. However, the diminutive detention centre isn't

The _____est Construction

without its detractors. Over five hours west of Tweed, in the village of Creemore, Ontario, stands another junior jailhouse. In operation from 1892 to 1940, this three-celled, not-so-big-house measures 4.5 metres by six metres and claims to be **North America's Smallest Jail**. As for which pokey is the smallest, why don't we just leave that verdict up to the prisoners?

Construction Ahead

Slow down! You're approaching the **Lowest Point on a Public Road in Canada**. Located in the George Massey Tunnel, under the Fraser River near the Vancouver International Airport, this all-time low point is 20 metres below sea level.

The Wee White North

Get your magnifying glass and let's see if we can find the **Smallest City in Canada**. Oh, there it is, beside that thimble. Located in the southern portion of British Columbia in the Kootenay Boundary region, near the U.S. border, the itty-bitty city of Greenwood is home to around 625 citizens.

A Stack of World Records

Toronto's CN Tower stacks up world records as if they were pancakes. And while one of the record-setting flap-jackpots has been eaten up by another free-standing structure, the CN Tower's record collection is still as sweet. For more than 30 years, the CN Tower was considered the **World's Tallest Free-standing Structure**—meaning that it supports itself. Unfortunately, in 2007, while still under construction, the 818-metre-tall Burj

Khalifa in Dubai, United Arab Emirates, surpassed the CN Tower's still impressive 553-metre stature. As a consolation prize, the CN Tower is still the **Tallest Free-standing Structure in the Western Hemisphere**.

Bragging Rights

Stand tall, First Canadian Place in downtown Toronto, because you're the **Tallest Skyscraper in Canada**. At a towering 298 metres, First Canadian Place is the 11th tallest building in North America and the third tallest free-standing structure in Canada, after the CN Tower.

Sight CN

Even if the CN Tower is no longer considered the world's tallest free-standing structure, it still holds a number of other world records:

- At 447 metres, the Tower's Space Deck is the **World's Highest Public Observation Gallery**.
- With 2579 metallic steps, the Tower has the **World's Longest Metal Staircase**.
- Able to travel to a height of 346 metres, the Tower's elevator is the **World's Highest Glass-Floor Elevator**.
- At 351 metres, the Tower's 360 Restaurant is the **World's Highest Revolving Restaurant**.
- Inside 360 Restaurant is what used to be the **World's Highest Bar**, until it was beat by Shanghai's Cloud 9.
- At the same elevation and capable of holding up to 9000 bottles of wine, the Tower's "Cellar in the Sky" is the **World's Highest Wine Cellar**.

Construction Ahead

Slow down! You're approaching Lake Louise, Alberta. With an elevation of 1661 metres, it's the **Highest Town in Canada**.

Carry-on Baggage

Capable of reaching top speeds of almost Mach 2, the Avro Canada CF-105 Arrow had too much baggage to be cleared for takeoff. At the time of its construction during the 1950s, the Avro Arrow was considered to be the **World's Fastest Interceptor**. Unfortunately, shortly after the fighter craft began its flight-test simulations, the entire project was unexpectedly shut down by Canadian Prime Minister John Diefenbaker, who blamed out-of-control government spending.

With design costs of the aircraft reaching $10.2 million more than had originally been projected, in February 1959, the project was terminated, leaving over 14,000 Avro employees jobless. While the decision to terminate the interceptor initiative is considered to be a hot-button issue to this day, on the bright side, many of the engineers that worked on the Avro Arrow moved down south and helped establish the wildly success U.S. space program. Although the cancellation of the program saw all five test-flight models of the Avro Arrow destroyed, some of the aircraft's parts, such as the front nose section and cockpit, were saved and are currently on display at the Canada Aviation Museum in Ottawa.

Bragging Rights

Velocity Vessel

If the real explorer Marco Polo had a sailing vessel as speedy as the Canadian-constructed clipper ship named after him, he could have made it from Asia to Venice in record time. Constructed in the Courtenay Bay yards near St. John, New Brunswick, this three-masted wooden clipper-ship measured 56 metres long and weighed 1474 tonnes. Although the *Marco Polo* was designed to carry cargo over the seven seas, in 1852, it was converted into a passenger ship that transported travellers back and fourth between Liverpool, England and Australia. But serving as a passenger vessel did not diminish the ship's need for speed. That same year, the *Marco Polo* became the **World's Fastest Sailing Ship**. After a three-week layover Down Under, the *Marco Polo* departed for home. A trip from Australia to Liverpool would normally take other passenger vessels nearly nine months to complete, but the *Marco Polo* made the journey in a mere five months and 21 days.

In 1867, after being converted back to a cargo ship, the *Marco Polo* sprang a leak and sank off the shore of what is now Prince Edward Island National Park, where her remains still lie.

Treasured Trail

Be careful if you go hiking on the Trans-Canada Trail—
you may just end up in a different province. Proposed
in 1992 as a means of celebrating Canada's 125th birthday,
the Trans-Canada Trail, when completed, will be the
World's Longest Shared-Use Recreational Trail.

Expected to traverse every Canadian province and territory,
the trail is being built on existing walking trails and disused
rail corridors and will span over 22,000 kilometres.
Although it has been heavily funded through provincial
and federal dollars, donations by individual Canadians are
essential to the cause. A $50 donation gets a donor's name
linked to a metre of the trail. As of 2009, construction of
the Trans-Canada Trail is more than 70 percent complete.

Bragging Rights

Congratulations, Cape Spear
Lighthouse! Preventing ships from
crashing into Canada's east coast since
1836, **Canada's Most Eastern Point of
Light** was constructed from parts shipped over from
Scotland. The signal light is also considered to
be the **Oldest Surviving Lighthouse in
Newfoundland and Labrador**.

Reconstruction Site

Workers didn't have to worry about being electrocuted on
this historical jobsite, because Fortress Louisbourg didn't
have electricity. And, when labourers signed up to work
on the **World's Biggest Historical Reconstruction**, they
were required to learn 18th-century French masonry
techniques in order to return the fortress to its glory days.

Located in Louisbourg, Nova Scotia, the fortress was built
by French settlers in 1713 and survived many an attack

from British soldiers. Wear and tear over the centuries, however, took its toll on the ancient stronghold, so in 1961, the Canadian government announced that it would fund the reconstruction of one-quarter of the fortress, which has since been designated a National Historic Site.

construction Ahead

Slow down! You're approaching the Canso Causeway—the **World's Deepest Causeway**. Over 1385 metres long, the rock bridge, which connects Cape Breton Island to mainland Nova Scotia, consists of 10 million tonnes of rock that was quarried from a nearby mountain. The huge amount of rock was necessary because the Strait of Canso— the body of water that divides the two landmasses— had to be filled in to a depth of 65 metres.

Forever Yonge

Although it no longer holds the title of World's Longest Street, Toronto's Yonge Street is still the **Longest Street in Canada**.

Named after Sir George Yonge, Canadian Secretary of War, the 1896-kilometre-long thoroughfare stretches from Lake Ontario through central and northern Ontario, before ending at the Ontario-Minnesota border. Unfortunately, since Ontario's Highway 11 is no longer considered connected to Yonge Street, the record for world's longest street is currently unclaimed.

Bragging Rights

Power Falls

Taking nine years and over 30,000 workers to complete, the Twin Falls power station, located on the Churchill River in Newfoundland and Labrador, was **North America's Largest Civil Engineering Project** when it was constructed in 1963. A joint venture between Newfoundland and Hydro Québec, the electrical power plant cost $47.5 million to build. Today, that cost would be somewhere around the $950 million mark.

Yes, We're Still Open

Incorporated in 1929, the New Brunswick Museum got its start with a collection of rock and mineral displays. Today, the museum houses antiquities from around the world and is recognized as **Canada's Oldest Continuously Operating Museum**.

Arch Envy

With a height of 214 metres, a length of 1.3 kilometres and with 14 buttresses (brick supports that keep the dam walls from collapsing) the Daniel-Johnson Dam on the Manicouagan River outside Baie-Comeau, Québec, is the **World's Largest Multi-Arch Dam**.

Deep Feat

At 2206 metres below the surface, the Macassa Gold Mine in Kirkland Lake, Ontario, is the **Deepest Mine Shaft in Canada**.

Super Shush

Inaugurated in 1828 in downtown Montréal, the Atwater Library and Computer Centre is **Canada's Oldest Lending Library**. To clear up any confusion, the "Computer Centre" portion of the library was not established until much later, when the library had electricity.

U of Duh

Nicknamed STU and offering mostly undergraduate degrees in journalism and the liberal arts, St. Thomas University in Fredericton, New Brunswick, is considered the **Easiest University to Get Accepted to in Canada**.

The _____est Construction

Skill Building

1. How many cars did the longest passenger train in Canada have?
   A. 21 cars
   B. 31 cars
   C. 41 cars
   D. 51 cars

2. Where is the world's largest Olympic museum located?
   A. Vancouver
   B. Calgary
   C. Toronto
   D. Montréal

3. Where is Canada's oldest continuously used post office located?
   A. Ontario
   B. Nova Scotia
   C. Québec
   D. Yukon

4. Where is Canada's oldest operating lighthouse located?
   A. Manitoba
   B. Prince Edward Island
   C. Newfoundland and Labrador
   D. Nova Scotia

5. Which of the following is Canada's largest national park?
   A. Banff National Park
   B. Wood Buffalo National Park
   C. Prince Edward Island National Park
   D. International National Park

6. What is the largest university in Canada?
   A. University of British Columbia
   B. University of Alberta
   C. University of Toronto
   D. McGill University

7. Which province is the most densely populated?
   A. Ontario
   B. Nova Scotia
   C. New Brunswick
   D. Prince Edward Island

8. What is the largest city in Canada?
   A. Montréal
   B. Toronto
   C. Vancouver
   D. Winnipeg

9. What is the oldest chain store in Canada?
   A. The Bay
   B. Sears
   C. Walmart
   D. Uncle Link's Multi-purpose Chain Store

10. Which Saskatchewan city has the lowest elevation?
    A. Regina
    B. Moose Jaw
    C. Prince Albert
    D. Limbo

Answers on pages 241–42.

The _____est Construction

Skyscraper Scavenger Hunt

As part of a prank, Dalhousie University students have relocated the tallest buildings from each major Canadian city. As an architect, it is now your job to return each skyscraper to its proper place by drawing a line from the building to its corresponding city.

Yellowknife	Legislative Building of Nunavut
Halifax	Yukon Legislative Building
St. John's	Delta Prince Edward
Winnipeg	Assumption Place
Regina	La Renaissance Apartments
Toronto	1250 René-Lévesque
Calgary	Living Shangri-La
Montréal	Manulife Place
Vancouver	Suncor Energy Centre West
Edmonton	Delta Regina Hotel
Charlottetown	Canwest Place
Saskatoon	John Cabot Building
Moncton	Fenwick Place
Whitehorse	First Canadian Place
Nunavut	Centre Square

Answers on page 242.

Word Shambles

The following structural words have collapsed. Now, as a structural engineer, it is your job to sift through the rubble and reconstruct each word to its former glory before the cleaning crew arrives and starts hauling the letters to the dump.

SUDST _____

GRTOU _____

RORATM _____

NTIOJ _____

IRVCTLAE _____

IKBRC _____

ANSETEDF _____

AERFM _____

TLEI _____

LAWL _____

TITCA _____

VANOTTLEIRS _____

GYIHAHW _____

ADM _____

GIEBRD _____

RSRKCPASYE _____

YUWBAS _____

REPCILP _____

HCRCHU _____

NARB _____

Answers on page 242.

The _____est Construction

Building Acrossword

Your construction company has been short listed to head up the construction of the town's new underwater library. Before you and your bulldozers can move in, however, you must complete the following structural crossword.

ACROSS

2. Groundwork
3. Keeps cables in line
7. Heat retainer
8. For pedestrians only
10. A bridge's ability to hang
12. CN, for one
15. A quarterback's home
16. Underground area
17. A house on a fault line

DOWN

1. Where pigeons hang out
4. Construction main metal
5. Hammer hater
6. Roof supporter
8. Transparent pane
9. Lumber
11. Large-scale umbrella
13. Bringers of water
14. Compacted wire

Answers on page 242.

Concrete Jungle

A group of structure-related words went to Alphabet City on a school field trip. Unfortunately, while admiring the architecture, the words got lost among the mile-high letters and gleaming characters. Now, as the tour guide, it is your job to find the structure-related terms and return them back to school.

```
L A D A J B R A C I N G D A O L L C U T Y
L R E W E S E N R U A N O I S E O I T R R
A O O J D R Y W A L L I O Y A A O T I A N
W A P O O E R O B Y Y B R T E G J E L C O
Y D H I L B E T A E R M S R G N O G Y Y S
R S A S U F D E N A N U O E E W I N E A A
U T L T N L E V A R G L O T C O N Y A W M
N U T S I N Y A L J D P L F S D T E T L T
I L E R V K A N Y O I J E A T J S L S I I
V A S P H A L T S I A D Y R Y O E L R A C
E T B L E C I E I S G C T S U I A O E R O
R Y R O O L F F T W F L I A R T Y C K C W
S O U K I E O J Y B O A L E K K C D A E N
I O N T C O N T R A C T O R C N A U E S L
T R U H R A E I E D S T E L A A E L R R O
Y Y J A G D K C H A N N E L W K N A B T A
E E G E L L O C D B A C K A E L O O H C S
```

Utility	Floor	Doors	City
Sewer	Bracing	Trail	Town
Plumbing	Joists	Roads	Joint
Contractor	Rafter	Railway	Load
Floor	Asphalt	School	Masonry
Structure	Gravel	Bank	Channel
Breaker	Roof	University	
Diagonal	Drywall	College	

The _____est Construction

The ____est Marvels

Biggest	*Scariest*
Hairiest	*Tastiest*
Tallest	*Heaviest*
Smallest	*Fastest*
Oldest	*Youngest*
Deadliest	*Dumbest*
Mushiest	*Chubbiest*
Loudest	*Fattest*
Stickiest	*Strangest*

(Superlative recommendations for chapter title—pick one or add your own)

Canadian Idols

It's no secret that Canada is obsessed with constructing immense marvels of all types. The country is littered with super-sized shrines honouring some truly bizarre things, such as a giant perogy and a moose the size of a caboose. And although some people may think this habit of ours is foolish, our dedication to mammoth and micro-sized monuments doesn't mean we're crazy—Canada builds large and little landmarks to commemorate its past accomplishments, as well as to protect its future from giant monster attacks. Think about it, a rampaging cyclops would be too distracted by the world's largest cowboy boot to destroy the city of Edmonton.

The country is prepared for monster mêlées in other ways, too. For example, why would a leviathan from the ocean depths want to chew on a Newfie, when it could munch down on the world's largest piece of fudge or slurp the country's biggest smoothie? If the food doesn't subdue invaders, then the world's longest hula or the world's biggest car wash will certainly distract an agitated giant gorilla long enough for the army to move into position. Believe it or not, Canada's bevy of big and small wonders will be its saving grace in the face of a nuclear or a monster attack.

But seriously, as we patiently wait for that fateful day, sightseers from around the globe continue to flock to Canada to see all its marvels, before they are destroyed.

19th-Century Toys R Us

Do you want to attract a boodle (a crowd of people) at recess this trimester? Then don't head back to the school-house without a bilbo catcher (cup and ball), a rolling hoop (hoop and stick) or a freshly shucked corn doll. They are all included in the Percy Band Toy Collection in Toronto's Black Creek Pioneer Museum.

With over 2000 toys and games that span the 1800s, the Percy Band Toy Collection is **Canada's Largest Collection of 19th-Century Toys**. This colossal assortment of low-tech gizmos, gadgets and street games such as jacks and jump rope started with a generous donation from area resident Percy Snider in 1954. And it has continued to grow ever since.

While the toy collection is now in the museum at the Black Creek Pioneer Village, it was formerly in the Dalziel Barn Museum, a 762-square-metre Pennsylvania-style barn that was the cornerstone of what would eventually become the living-history park. Recognized as **Canada's First Agricultural Museum**, the Dalziel Barn Museum is also considered the **Oldest Pennsylvania Barn in the World** and the **Largest Pennsylvania Barn in North America**. This antique barn is still located on its original site, with its original foundation still intact.

Canadian Curiosities

On Canada Day, July 1, 2001, Industrial Thermo Polymers Ltd. in Brampton, Ontario, strung together hundreds of pool noodles for a total length of 1609.34 metres, creating the **World's Longest Pool Toy**.

Word Up

The word on the street is that Canada's Inuit people have over 100 words for "snow," making it the **Word with the Most Meanings**. For example, the first snowfall of autumn is called *apigianngaut*, while melting snow in spring is called *mannsguq*. Snowing for making water with is called *aniu*, and *aput* describes snow that is found on the ground. Plus, instead of catching "snowflakes" on their tongues, the Inuit catch *qannik*. Surprisingly, while they have an overabundance of words for the cold, white stuff, the Inuit people have no word for "goodbye."

Instrumental Feat

At Vancouver's BC Place on May 15, 2000, Vancouver Symphony Orchestra maestro Bramwell Tovey and 6452 musicians clinched the record for the **World's Largest Orchestra**.

Crazy Train

In the mid-1930s, during its regular run from Montréal to Smith Falls, Ontario, a Canadian Pacific Railway F-2a engine clocked in at 180 kilometres per hour, giving it the record for the **Highest Speed for a Steam Locomotive in Canada**.

Now That's a Big...
Slab of Fudge

You'll need a whole new set of teeth after experiencing the cavity-inducing excitement of the **World's Largest Slab of Fudge**. Designed by the Northwest Fudge Factory in Levack, Ontario, for the 2004 FedNor Pavilion at the Royal Winter Fair in Toronto, this fat slab of fudge measured approximately 14 metres long, two metres wide and 10 centimetres thick and weighed 2290 kilograms (over two tonnes!). For the record, the flavour of the fudge was creamy vanilla chocolate.

Non-perishable Charity

Lending a helping hand is a Canadian trait, so it's no wonder that Canada holds a record for kindness. On April 14, 2008, the Greater Toronto Apartment Association managed to collect 119,068 kilograms of non-perishable food items for the Toronto Daily Bread Food Bank. That outpouring of generosity set the world record for the **Most Food Donated in 24 Hours**. The previous record was set two years prior in Regina, where volunteers collected 100,244 kilograms of food.

Extra! Extra!

Read all about it! Winnipeg media mogul Israel "Izzy" Asper inks **Biggest Media Deal in Canadian History**.

In 2000, the founder of the CanWest Global Communications Corporation purchased the majority of Conrad

Black's shares in the *National Post* newspaper, as well as 13 other major and 136 smaller newspapers around the world, for $3.5 billion.

Canadian Curiosities

During Hanukkah in 2008, 22-year-old "Furious" Pete Czerwinski of Toronto, Ontario, set the world record for the **Most Latkes Eaten in Eight Minutes**. In total, Czerwinski ate 46 latkes (potato pancakes). He also owns the world record for the **Most Bananas Consumed in Two Minutes**—18.

Show Me the Way

What's that up ahead? It's the **World's Tallest Inukshuk**—a human-built stone landmark used by the Inuit for navigation and to mark hunting grounds and places of respect. Measuring an impressive 11.9 metres in height and weighing over 80 tonnes, this particular inukshuk is located in Schomberg, Ontario, and was constructed out of 11 pieces of solid granite. It stands nearly three metres taller than its closest competitor in Vancouver, which dates from Expo '86.

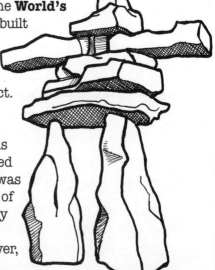

Final Destination

On September 2, 1998, Swissair Flight 111 departed from New York City's John F. Kennedy International Airport on its way to Switzerland. Unfortunately, the plane and its 229 passengers never made it to their final destination. En route to Switzerland, a fire broke out aboard the aircraft, forcing the McDonnell Douglas MD-11 to crash in the Atlantic Ocean off the coast of Peggy's Cove, Nova Scotia. The investigation into the accident took four years to complete and cost approximately $57 million. It was the **Worst Air Accident in Canadian History** and the **Highest-ever Death Toll Involving a McDonnell Douglas MD-11**.

Now That's a Big...
Pontoon operation

With a fleet of over 30 floatplanes that service Victoria, Nanaimo, Vancouver and the Gulf Islands, Harbour Air in Richmond, British Columbia, is the **World's Largest All-Seaplane Airline**.

De-Railway

The **Worst Train Wreck in Canadian History** could have been avoided, if only the conductor had obeyed all posted traffic signs.

On June 29, 1864, near what is now Mont-Saint-Hilaire, Québec, a train carrying mostly Polish and German immigrants ignored a stop sign while approaching a swing bridge—a moveable bridge that pivots, allowing cargo ships to pass by—and subsequently fell into the Richelieu River. Ninety-nine passengers lost their lives that day in what would become known as the St-Hilaire Train Disaster.

The House that Anne Built

Although she didn't "technically" build the quaint two-storey farmhouse with green gables situated above the window fixtures, Anne Shirley certainly did help to make the homestead **Prince Edward Island's Biggest Tourist Attraction**. Located in Cavendish, Prince Edward Island, the tiny farmhouse served as the setting for area writer Lucy Maud Montgomery's timeless novel *Anne of Green Gables*.

The farmhouse was owned by her cousins, and Montgomery would often visit as a child. Later, upon Montgomery's death, her wake was held in the living room of Green Gables. Every year, thousands of Anne fans from around the world visit Green Gables, which is now the property of the Government of Canada. In 2008, *Anne of Green Gables* celebrated its 100th anniversary of publication.

Now That's a Big... Burl

A burl is a knotty wart or lump found on the side of a tree, and Port McNeill, British Columbia, is home to the **World's Biggest Burl**. Measuring six metres tall and six metres wide, this big burl weighs 27 tonnes.

Harbour Horror

Halifax Harbour is recognized as one of the deepest and largest natural harbours in the world, but its true claim to fame is of a much more gruesome nature. At the time it occurred, the Halifax Explosion was the **Greatest Human-Created Blast Before Hiroshima**.

On the morning of December 6, 1917, a Belgian ship sailing in the harbour collided with a French munitions carrier that was hauling 2270 tonnes of TNT. The resulting explosion created a giant fireball that rose nearly two kilometres into the air and created a tsunami that rose 18 metres above the harbour's high-water mark. The blast decimated 2.5 square kilometres of Halifax, killing 1000 people and leaving 25,000 homeless. The explosion was so intense that it shook the windows of buildings over 16 kilometres away. While the title of greatest human-made blast was handed over to the Americans in 1945 when they bombed Hiroshima, Japan, the Halifax incident is still considered to be the **World's Largest Human-Made Accidental Explosion**.

Canadian curiosities

With over 2.9 million members worldwide, Vancouver-founded Greenpeace is the **World's Largest Environmental Organization**.

Trolley Death Toll

When commuters crammed their way onto the overcrowded streetcar on May 26, 1896, they paid the trolley toll with their lives.

As the packed streetcar was crossing Point Ellice Bridge in Victoria, British Columbia, the tremendous weight of the passengers aboard the trolley caused the bridge to give way, sending the streetcar plunging into the murky waters below. Fifty-five people lost their lives that day, making it the **Worst Streetcar Accident in North America**.

Canadian Curiosities

On February 15, 2008, Guinness World Records was sold to the Jim Pattison Group, the **Third Largest Private Company in Canada**.

Old News

The *Halifax Gazette* has been lining the bottoms of birdcages longer than any other Canadian newspaper. First published on March 23, 1752, the *Halifax Gazette* is considered to be the **Oldest Newspaper in Canada**. Published weekly until 1867, the *Gazette* was renamed the *Nova Scotia Royal Gazette* that year and is now the official publication of laws and legislations for the Government of Nova Scotia.

Skip To My Woo Hoo!

On May 29, 2005, Chris Brown skipped the entire length of the ING Ottawa Marathon in four hours, 49 minutes and 39 seconds—the **World's Fastest Time to Skip a Marathon**.

Bragging Rights

In 2006, Glencoe, Ontario's McEachren Family Farm designed **Canada's Largest Corn Maze**. Measuring 9.5 hectares, the lengthy labyrinth stretched over 20 football fields long and was dedicated to Muscular Dystrophy Canada.

License to Growl

Boasting **North America's Only Non-Rectangular Licence Plate**, the Northwest Territories think outside the box. In 1970, to celebrate its centennial, the Northwest Territories government held a competition among all its schools to design a new licence plate for the territory. The winning design was a blue-and-white plate in the shape of a polar bear and was based on a concept submitted by a high school student from Yellowknife.

Best Two Out of Three

On April 3, 2009, approximately 1150 students from Colonel By Secondary School in Ottawa, Ontario took part in the **World's Largest Rock-Paper-Scissors Tournament**.

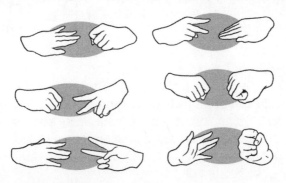

A Hard Chorus Line

In November 2006, citizens of Toronto kicked their way into the record books by assembling the **World's Longest Single Line of Dancers**. The dance group, which consisted of more than 1681 Torontonians, along with a number of leggy Rockettes from Radio City Music Hall, performed a kick line down Yonge Street for five minutes non-stop.

Jazz Feat

Founded in 1979, the Festival International de Jazz de Montréal is the **World's Largest Jazz Festival**. Every July, the event now attracts over 2,000,000 cool cats and kitties.

Must-Read TV

You would have needed a lot more than luck to win **Canada's Longest Running Weekly TV Show**. A current-affairs game show in which journalists attempted to guess the news story by asking a secret guest an array of questions, *Front Page Challenge* aired from 1957 to 1985. During its 38-year run on CBC-TV, *Front Page Challenge* welcomed many notable secret guests to its stage, including human-rights activist Malcolm X, variety-show host Ed Sullivan, India's Prime Minister Indira Gandhi, hockey legend Gordie Howe and horror movie staple Boris Karloff, who answered questions pertaining to the 1912 Regina Cyclone, where he had worked as a rescue volunteer.

Bragging Rights

Guardian Snow Angels

On February 2, 2004, as a tribute to a district administrator who was ill, teachers, students, administrators and parents from about 60 schools within London, Ontario's District Catholic School Board simultaneously lay down in the cold, wet snow and made 15,851 snow angels—the **Most Snow Angels Made at Once**.

Temporary Tree

On September 21, 1993, in Harrison Hot Springs, British Columbia, a 6.3-metre-high Christmas tree constructed entirely out of sand was unveiled. At the time of its completion, it was the **World's Largest Sand Sculpture**.

Now That's a Big . . .
Ball of Tape

On June 18, 2006, Tim Funk and his 12-year-old son, Ryan, from Langley, British Columbia, unveiled a ball of adhesive tape—consisting mostly of hockey tape (shin and stick) donated by teams across Canada—with a circumference of 7.23 metres that weighed 844.59 kilograms— the **World's Largest Ball of Adhesive Tape**.

A Tall Night's Sleep

Authentic princesses, narcoleptics and jumping monkeys around the world should be interested in this next record. On August 26, 2006, members of the Whitby, Ontario, Rotary Club piled a stack of mattresses 3.6 metres high to make what was at the time the **World's Tallest Stack of Mattresses**. There's no word on whether or not they laid down a pea before construction commenced.

Seniors Hotline

If you ever want make a call to the **World's Oldest Telephone Kiosk**, call Salmo, British Columbia. Carved into the stump of a 465-year-old cedar tree, this way-past-its-prime phone booth is still relaying messages from outside the Sal-Crest Motel in downtown Salmo.

Jelly-filled Joy

Selling more than three million doughnuts per day, Tim Hortons is **Canada's Leading Doughnut Chain**. Doughnuts are also the **Most Popular Food in Canada**.

A Big-Ticket Item

Can you imagine the size of the ticket stub? On February 8, 2007, the National Arts Centre in Ottawa, Ontario, unveiled the **World's Largest Admission Ticket**. Designed by a graphics firm from Saskatoon, Saskatchewan, the substantial soon-to-be stub measured 142 centimetres in length by 50 centimetres in width—10 times the size of a regular concert ticket. The irregularly sized receipt was a promotional vehicle for an upcoming National Arts Centre Orchestra concert. The voluminous voucher also marked the first entry in the *Guinness Book of Records* oversized admission ticket category.

Now That's a Big...
Rutabaga

Cannington, Ontario's Norm Craven currently holds the record for growing the **World's Largest Rutabaga**. In total, Craven's gargantuan yellow turnip weighed 35 kilograms and was almost twice the size of a human head.

Signpost-Its

Although interesting, this record sparks a question: Who walks around with a signpost?

Every year, thousands of tourists from around the world add anywhere from 2500 to 4000 new signposts (information or directional signs from different parts of the world)

to Watson Lake, Yukon's Sign Post Forest. The **World's Largest Collection of Signposts** was born out of a homesick U.S. soldier's yearning to be back in Danville, Illinois. Far away from home while working on the Alaska Highway, the wistful officer planted the forest's very first signpost in 1942. By 1990, the forest had grown to over 10,000 signposts. The last time anyone counted them, the number had ballooned to over 65,000.

Canadian curiosities

Cape St. George-Petit Jardin-Grand Jardin-De Grau-Marches Point-Loretto, Newfoundland and Labrador, is the **Longest Place Name in Canada**.

P.S. Watch Out for Icebergs

While most letters aren't worth the stamp it costs to send them, one particular correspondence dispatched from the famed *Titanic* turned out to be the **Most Expensive Letter Written by a Canadian**.

Dated April 10, 1912—two days before the ship sank off the coast of Newfoundland—the note was written by *Titanic* passenger George Graham of Harriston, Ontario, a sales manager with Eaton's department store. The correspondence was addressed to Graham's colleague in Berlin, Germany, and was mailed the morning that the *Titanic* departed on its maiden voyage across the North Atlantic. In February 2009, the letter sold at auction in New York for the titanic sum of $16,100.

Now That's a Big...
Gold Coin

Created by the Royal Canadian Mint in Ottawa, Ontario, on May 3, 2007, the **World's Largest Gold Coin** weighs 100 kilograms and has a diameter of 50 centimetres and a thickness of three centimetres. Minted from gold with a purity of 99.999 percent, the colossal coin has a face value of $ 1 million.

Extra Overtime

Covering its first faceoff via radio in 1931, *Hockey Night in Canada* made the transition to CBC television in the fall of 1952. Almost 80 years later, *Hockey Night in Canada* is the **World's Oldest Sports-Related Program Still On Air**.

Televised in both official languages, English and French, it features a weekly instalment of "Coach's Corner," hosted by Don Cherry and Ron MacLean. The only thing that has changed over the last seven decades is the theme song. After losing the rights to the legendary song in 2008, the CBC held a nationwide contest to find a replacement tune. With thousands of songs submitted, the network settled on the theme song titled "Canadian Gold," which was composed by a schoolteacher from Edmonton.

Addicted to Hugs

Staff and students in Ottawa have a serious hugging problem.

On April 25, 2008, over 10,000 students and teachers from 10 Ottawa-area schools hugged it out for the **World's Largest Group Hug** record. A volunteer effort to raise funds for cancer research, the huggers squeezed out more than $150,000 for the cause.

Nerd Feat

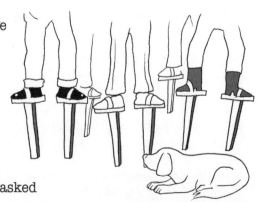

On October 22, 2005, Montréaler Dwayne Richard reached 473,400 points in Donkey Kong 3—the **World's Highest Score in a Classic Arcade Game**.

The Height of Excitement

When members of Montréal's Cirque du Soleil stepped into the record books at an altitude of 33 centimetres above the ground, it was not to change light bulbs, clean out the gutters or reach something on the top shelf, it was to mark the organization's 25th anniversary.

On June 16, 2009, Cirque organizers asked

performers from around the world to meet on stilts and help them set the world record for the **Most People Walking on Stilts Simultaneously**. And they did. In Montréal alone, over 900 people walked 100 metres on 33-centimetre-tall stilts.

Canadian curiosities

Saskatoon, Saskatchewan's Sundog Handcraft Faire is **Western Canada's Largest Craft Fair**.

What a Ding-Dong

Hear ye! Hear ye! From July 25 to 26, 2005, Joe Defries of Penticton, British Columbia, rang a handheld bell for 28 hours and 50 minutes—the **World's Longest Bell Ringing**.

Wheel Good

From September 8 to 9, 2006, a 10-member team of gymnasts from Memramcook, New Brunswick, cartwheeled 50 kilometres in one day—the **World's Greatest Distance Travelled in 24-Hours by a Team Performing Cartwheels**.

Around the World in 60 Minutes

Yo-yo, listen up, on July 14, 1990, "Fast" Eddy McDonald of Cavendish, Prince Edward Island, performed the **Most Yo-Yo Loops in One Hour**—8437.

Tickle Trunk Triumph

Who would have thought that a television show that featured a grown man talking to a pair of hand puppets would be so successful? Airing from 1967 to 1996, CBC's *Mr. Dressup*, starring Ernie Coombs and his puppet friends Casey and Finnegan, is the **Longest Running Children's Program Television in Canada**.

Canadian Curiosities

The Toronto International Film Festival is the **World's Largest Publicly Attended Film Festival**.

Logging On

Another unlikely Canadian television success was a show about collecting wayward logs.

Airing from 1972 to 1990, CBC's *The Beachcombers*, starring Bruno Gerussi as a West Coast log salvager, is the **Longest Running Dramatic Television Program in Canada**.

The Human Hole

With so many holes in his body, Winnipeg, Manitoba's Brent Moffat should definitely avoid swimming. The current holder of the record for the **World's Most Body Piercings with Surgical Instruments**, in January 2002, Moffat, whose nickname is the "Human Pincushion," inserted 702 needles into his body over the span of eight hours. Moffatt's attempt demolished the previous record of 200 piercings, set back in 1999.

Bragging Rights

Walk the dog, Cedarview Middle School in Ottawa, Ontario! You hold the record for the **World's Largest Simultaneous Yo-Yo Event**. Set on June 8, 2006, the event saw 432 people yo-yo at the same time, beating the previous record set by 426 people in Dublin, Ireland, in 2002.

November Shame

Violence and bloodshed in General Motors Place is unheard of—especially on a night that the Vancouver Canucks aren't playing. So it was surprising that "The Garage" was the site of the **Worst Riot in Canadian History**. On November 7, 2002, the opening night of Guns N' Roses' Chinese Democracy tour, fans of the heavy-metal act lost their cool.

The concert was set to commence at 9:30 PM, but at 8:00 PM, the 8000 or so head-bangers who had congregated outside GM Place received word that Axl Rose, the singer and sole surviving original member of the group, had cancelled the night's performance because of "health reasons."

Before the cancellation announcement was finished, fans had already begun overturning flower planters and garbage cans, using them to smash out the windows of the Vancouver venue. When police arrived on the scene, rioters redirected their aggression from dismantling the arena to attacking the law enforcement officers. Although officers took a few lumps from the protesters, in the end, they got the upper hand, keeping civilian injuries to a minimum and arresting 12 people in the process. In total, the rock 'n' rioters caused $350,000 in property damage. What's ironic about the whole ordeal was the fact that Axl Rose—the target of the mob's anger—was not in the arena at the time of the uprising. As it turned out, he had never even left Los Angeles.

Look Up, Way Up

Measuring 38.8 metres in height, **Canada's Tallest Totem Pole** (built from a single log) was erected in Beacon Hill Park in Victoria, British Columbia, in 1956. In First Nations cultures, totem poles have varied meanings, but most totems are designed to recount local legends and notable tribal events. The Beacon Hill Park totem pole is the fourth largest in the world.

Now That's a Big...
Tomahawk

Cut Knife, Saskatchewan, is home to the **World's Largest Tomahawk**. Measuring 11.8 metres high and weighing six tonnes, the titanic tomahawk, which rests on a gigantic tipi, was built in 1971 as a symbol of unity and friendship between the First Nations people and the other residents of Cut Knife.

Fire Walk of Fame

Mmm, something smells like Kentucky Fried Feet. On June 15, 2005, Grande Prairie, Alberta, native Amanda Dennison walked 67 metres over glowing embers radiating between 870 and 980 degrees Celsius to earn the record for the **World's Longest Fire Walk**. The previous record was 51 metres.

Big Gulp

According to Guinness World Records, an unknown Canadian woman holds the title of the **World's Most Compulsive Swallower**, which she set back in 1927. While details surrounding the woman's identity are sketchy, she is credited with having over 2533 items removed from her stomach, including more than 945 pins.

Speech Feat

In 1995, Canada's Sean Shannon was declared the **World's Fastest Talker** after he recited the 260-word "To Be or Not To Be" soliloquy from Shakespeare's *Hamlet* in 23.8 seconds.

Nuclear Missive

Before the days of texts, tweets and telephones—they had telephones in 1969, but they were rotary and didn't have Internet capability, so they don't count—people had to send messages via telegram. And not the fun kind of telegram, like a singing one, but a boring text-heavy telegram, written on a piece of paper.

In protest of the U.S. Department of Energy's underground testing of nuclear arms on the Aleutian Island of Amchitka, located in extreme southwestern Alaska, peace-minded Canadians sent the **World's Longest Telegram** to Washington, DC. Sent on November 1, 1969, the petition was signed by 177,000 Canadians, measured one kilometre long and took Western Union four days to deliver. Unfortunately, the Canadian concern mattered little to then U.S. President Richard Nixon. Nuclear testing on the island lasted until 1971, when it culminated with the detonation of U.S.'s largest underground nuclear explosion to date.

Canadian curiosities

The **World's Longest Uninterrupted Corridor of Cellular Telephone Service** stretches approximately 2345 kilometres from Windsor, Ontario, to Sydney, Nova Scotia.

It's for You

The Canadian inventor of the telephone, Alexander Graham Bell, referred to his innovative contraption as the **World's Rudest Instrument**, since it would regularly disrupt people during dinner, in the bath or while they were sleeping.

Drenched From Above!

That had better only be water in there. To celebrate its bicentennial, on June 20, 2005, Fort Nelson, British Columbia, staged the **World's Largest Water Balloon Fight**.

With volunteers filling 3000 balloons per hour, the inflatable artillery was then stored in cardboard flats and placed in the back of six pickup trunks for safekeeping. When it came time to toss the bulbous bags, residents did so in record time and quantity. Tossing 40,000 water-filled balloons in 3.5 minutes, Fort Nelson residents surpassed the previous record of 23,000 water balloons set by the town of Fishers, Indiana, on June 13, 2005. Students in the UK have since blasted our record.

Canadian Curiosities

Vancouver, British Columbia's BC Place is the **World's Largest Air-Supported Domed Stadium.**

Chopstick Handling

Fort Nelson, British Columbia, may not be the Chinese food capital of Canada, but it sure is the capital of Chinese food utensils. Producing over seven million pairs of chopsticks a day, Fort Nelson's Canadian Chopstick Manufacturing Company is the **World's Largest Chopstick Factory**.

Is Your Computer Running?

Is your computer is running? Then you had better catch it. But if it's **Canada's Fastest Computer** you're chasing, good luck.

Built by IBM and located at the University of Toronto, this supercomputer cost $50 million to build. Switched on in June 2009, the machine is able to process more than 300 trillion calculations per second. At peak consumption, it gobbles up the same amount of energy as 4000 homes, and data streams through its digital pathways at a rate equal to about two DVD movies per second. About 30 times more powerful than the next fastest research computer in Canada, this intimidating terminal is among the 15 fastest computers in the world.

Wheelin' Along

Way to roll, Brian Rhodes and John Cortes of Richmond, British Columbia, you hold the **World's Fastest Time for a One-mile (1.6 km) Wheelbarrow Race**. In 1980, at the Ladner Centennial Sports Festival in Delta, British Columbia, the pair completed the race in four minutes and 52 seconds.

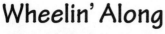

Knotty, Knotty

It's a good idea to always have a Boy Scout nearby, especially for those times when you fall down a crevasse and need a quick way out. On October 20, 2007, 325 Boy Scouts in Bowmanville, Ontario, constructed a rope chain that measured 1675 metres in record time—the **Longest Knotted Rope Chain Created in Five Minutes**.

Elf Feat

Retired geography teacher Jean-Guy Laquerre from Boucherville, Québec, owns more than 20,000 Santa Claus–related items, including illustrations and figurines, giving him the record for the **World's Largest Collection of Santa Claus Memorabilia**.

Solar Power Trip

While night driving is definitely not an option for the Midnight Sun Solar Car Team, they did manage to burn enough daylight to secure the title of **World's Longest Journey by a Solar Electric Vehicle**.

The team of University of Waterloo engineering students and their eco-friendly, four-wheel vehicle departed from Waterloo, Ontario, on August 7, 2004. Travelling a distance of 15,070 kilometres across Canada and through the United States, the team ended their journey on September 15, 2004, on Parliament Hill in Ottawa.

Speed Sketching

Carpal tunnel syndrome must be commonplace at Montréal's KliK Animation, the current titleholder of the **World's Fastest TV Animation Production**. From script to screen, it took animators six hours to render a one-minute animation piece titled *Le JourNul de François Pérusse (The Lame News by François Pérusse)*, which debuted on February 8, 1999, directly following the six o'clock news.

Now That's a Big...
Concert

From November 16 to 18, 1984, the King of Pop, Michael Jackson, played three back-to-back concerts at BC Place in Vancouver. Combined, a total of 110,000 people attended the concerts over the three nights, making it the **Biggest Concert in British Columbia**.

The Milky Way

Thirsty babies and their mothers throughout British Columbia gathered on October 6, 2001, to stage the **World's Largest Simultaneous Breastfeeding**.

Designed to draw attention to the benefits of breastfeeding, the event was held in 26 locations throughout the province and saw 793 nursing mothers and their suckling babes participate in the mass milking.

Canadian Curiosities

Saskatoon, Saskatchewan's Vesna Festival is home to the **World's Largest Ukrainian Cabaret**.

The _____est Marvels

That's a Hot Wax

On June 20, 2009, CARSTAR Automotive Canada in Hamilton, Ontario, entered the record books as the titleholder of the **World's Largest Car Wash Event**. The organization beat the previous record of 4000 washed cars by a record-breaking 2000 cars.

Paint By Big Numbers

The **Most Expensive Canadian Painting Ever Sold at Auction** was "Scene in the Northwest—Portrait" painted by Paul Kane in about 1845. It sold at auction for $5,062,500 in 2002.

Batter Up

Montréaler Bob Blumer, the host of Food Network's *The Surreal Gourmet* and *Glutton for Punishment*, is the current record holder of the **World's Most Flapjacks Made in One Hour**. On July 10, during the 2008 Calgary Stampede, Blumer made a batch of 559 pancakes in the span of 60 minutes.

Sticky Feat

Supplying 85 percent of the world's favourite tree sap concentrate, **Canada is the World's Largest Producer of Maple Syrup**. In 2004 alone, the country produced 26.8 million litres of the golden goo, which was valued at $149 million.

You Can't Catch Me!

You'll have a difficult time biting the head off the **World's Largest Gingerbread Man**. Measuring four metres in height and weighing 169 kilograms, the domineering doughboy was created in November 2003 by the Vancouver Hyatt Regency Hotel using 100 kilograms of flour, 20 kilograms of shortening, 20 kilograms of sugar and 20 kilograms of molasses.

Cracked Records

Scrambling to raise funds for the fight against asthma, the Ontario Lung Association made the **World's Largest Omelette**. In May 2002, using a specially designed frying pan that measured 13 metres in diameter, the Lung Association turned 165,000 eggs into a 2.7-tonne omelette.

Canadian Curiosities

Singer Céline Dion of Charlemagne, Québec, has the **Most Platinum and Multi-Platinum Albums in Canada**, a total of 24.

Tiny Torpedo

Although it isn't armed with nuclear weapons, Montréaler Pierre Poulin's miniature underwater vessel is
the **World's Smallest Submarine**. Weighing 620 kilograms, this one-person vehicle took its inaugural dive on
June 26, 2005, on Québec's Lake Memphrémagog.

Roll Out the Barrel

After watching the **World's Largest Accordion Ensemble**, you'd probably want to polka your eyes out. Fortunately, their were no such incidents at the 29th Annual
Newfoundland and Labrador Festival, where, on August 6,
2005, the assembled 989 accordion players squeezed
their way into the record books.

Aloha-ha!

Just because Canada doesn't have
palm trees, hot weather or erupt-
ing volcanoes doesn't mean that it
can't hold the record for the **World's
Largest Hula Dance**. On June 4, 2005,
at the annual Rose Festival in Welland,
Ontario, 122 dancers performed a hula.

Lifetime Subscription

When you have been delivering newspapers as long
as Velmore Smith has, they call you a paperman.
Supplying folks with the special edition since 1958,
Smith holds the record for the **World's Longest
Working Career**. When he retired in 2006, Smith had
been a paperboy for 44 years.

Canadian curiosities

The 35-minute round trip across Kootenay Lake, British Columbia, is believed to be the **World's Longest Free Ferry Ride.**

Five Letter Word for "Big"

"Large" certainly was the word that inspired Robert Turcot of Québec back in 1982 when he created the **World's Largest Published Crossword Puzzle.** Consisting of 82,951 squares, the gargantuan game contained 12,489 across clues and 13,125 down clues. When printed, the puzzle covered 3.55 square metres.

Canadian curiosities

The **Largest Repertory Theatre in North America** is located in Stratford, Ontario.

Break a Leg Already

Debuting on March 21, 1979, the play Broue (Brew), performed by Canada's Michel Côté, Marcel Gauthier and Marc Messier, is still running—30 years later—making it the **World's Longest Running Theatrical Play with the Same Cast.**

Sweatin' to the Hi-Tech

On May 22, 2009, in Burnaby, British Columbia, over 605 spandex-clad fitness fans celebrated the launch of Electronic Arts' Sports Active video game for the Nintendo Wii system by participating in the **World's Largest Simultaneous Video Game Exercise Routine**.

Underground Radio

Although CBC Radio's *Points North* is in no way an "underground radio show," on May 24, 2005, it literally aired from under the ground. Broadcasting from the Creight Mine in Sudbury, Ontario, 2340 metres underground, the two-hour-long, general-interest program claimed the title of the **World's Lowest Live Radio Broadcast**.

Carving Out a Record

Nova Scotia's Howard Dill has mutant pumpkin growing down to a science. After studying plant genetics, he developed a seed variety called Atlantic Giant in order to harvest a ginormous gourd, which he managed to do in 1982. Dill carved the massive marvel, which weighed 202 kilograms and had a circumference of three metres, into the **World's Largest Jack-O-Lantern**. Dill's reputation for growing "plumpkins" is said to have been the inspiration for Nova Scotia's annual Pumpkin Regatta—the **World's Largest and Longest Running Pumpkin Race**. Held since 1994, the Regatta sees contestants racing giant, hollowed-out, motor- or paddle-powered pumpkins a distance of 0.8 kilometres across Nova Scotia's Lake Pesaquid.

Guitar Heroes

Turn up the volume! On June 6, 2009, a throng of 1623 guitar players descended upon Toronto's Yonge-Dundas Square to strum Neil Young's song "Helpless" simultaneously. Although the group's attempt was shy of the world record, the strummers did manage to set a new record for **Canada's Largest Guitar Ensemble**.

Zombience

Brains! On October 29, 2006, Harbourfront Community Centre in Toronto hosted 62 decaying zombies, who danced their rotting carcasses into the record books by performing the **World's Largest "Thriller" Dance**.

Now That's a Big...
Dance Class

On September 12, 2008, staff and students of Ryerson University in Toronto took part in the **World's Largest Dance Class**. Over 626 participants busted moves to Jamiroquai's "Canned Heat" for 10 minutes. The attempt not only broke a sweat, but also the previously held dance record, which had been set by 580 dancers in Birmingham, England, earlier that year.

Never on a Sundae

On July 24, 1988, during Klondike Days in Edmonton, Alberta, the **World's Largest Ice Cream Sundae** was assembled using 20,100 kilograms of ice cream, 4260 kilograms of toppings, 90 kilograms of whipped cream, 50 kilograms of peanuts and 50 kilograms of cherries.

Food Feat

The Calgary Italian Bakery holds the world record for the **Largest Baked Loaf of Bread**. Measuring 2.75 metres by 1.5 metres, the loaf weighed 1384 kilograms.

Life in a Bubble

While most people hate living in a bubble, they don't seem to mind when it's for a world record. On December 16, 2006, Canadian Ana Yang fit 26 people inside a giant soap bubble for, you guessed it, the record for the **Most People Inside a Soap Bubble**.

The Moose is Loose

Founded in 1867 and still owned by the Oland family, now in its sixth generation, Moosehead Breweries Ltd. is the **Largest Fully Canadian-owned Brewery** and **Canada's Oldest Independent Brewery**.

You Booze, You Lose...a Lot

In the 1900s, during the Northern Ontario gold rush, a prospector named Sandy McIntyre and his partners staked claims near Timmins that went on to produce $230 million in gold. Unfortunately for him, McIntyre had immediately sold his share in the mine for $25 worth of liquor, making that purchase **Canada's Most Expensive Drink**.

Sweet Feat

On July 22, 2006, a London, Ontario, Booster Juice outlet mixed up 681.92 litres of bananas, strawberries, sorbet, ice and fruit juice to create the **World's Largest Smoothie**.

King-Sized Canada

Going Cuckoo in Kimberley

Kimberley, British Columbia, is home to the **World's Largest Free-standing Cuckoo Clock**. Located in the city's downtown, the clock is approximately 4.5 metres in height and contains a life-size, lederhosen-clad Bavarian named Happy Hans, who emerges from inside the clock and yodels for tourists when fed a quarter.

At Ease, Soldier

Any army would be honoured to have this 10-metre-tall tin soldier in its ranks. Constructed out of stainless steel and with a time capsule stored inside, the **World's Biggest Tin Soldier** was built to commemorate the Royal Engineers, who established the city of New Westminster, British Columbia. For the record, the time capsule is scheduled to be opened in 2025.

It Was This Big...

Holy catfish! It's **Canada's Biggest Catfish**. Swimming upstream in Selkirk, Manitoba, the "Catfish Capital of the World," the statue of "Chuck the Channel Cat" stands 7.6 metres tall.

Java Jive

Wake up! It's the **World's Biggest Coffee Pot**. Percolating in Davidson, Saskatchewan, this giant java jar stands 7.3 metres tall and could hold 150,000 225-millilitre cups of real coffee.

The Apple of Your Eye

Hardcore! It's the **World's Biggest Apple**. A product of Colborne, Ontario, this formidable fruit stands almost four storeys tall and has an observation deck on top.

Big Savings

Breaking into the **World's Largest Piggy Bank** may just land you in the hospital. Found in Coleman, Alberta, this super-sized swine is constructed out of a discarded steam engine that was used to haul tonnes of coal out of area mines. All proceeds collected from the penny-saving pig go to the local Lions Club.

Going Quackers

Duck! It's the **World's Largest Mallard Duck**. Nesting in Andrew, Alberta, this crazy huge quacker weighs one tonne and has a wingspan of 7.2 metres.

Something to Sink Your Teeth Into

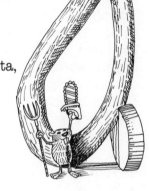

Nice to meat you, **World's Biggest Kielbasa**. Cured in Mundare, Alberta, this monstrous Ukrainian sausage stands 12.8 metres tall and weighs 5.5 tonnes. It cost $12,000 to build and can withstand winds of up to 160 kilometres per hour.

Rolling Along

Wagons, ho! It's the **World's Largest Wagon Wheel and Pick**. Hitched to a post in Fort Assiniboine, Manitoba, this wicked-big wagon stands 7.3 metres tall, while the kick-axe pick is six metres tall.

Monster Truck

Known as the Terex Titan, this titanic truck, which was built in London, Ontario, can hold two Greyhound buses inside its box. Measuring 20 metres long, eight metres wide and seven metres tall, the **World's Largest Truck** was originally designed to transport coal. The truck's maximum load is 350 tonnes. The Terex Titan is currently parked in Sparwood, British Columbia, where local police are too intimidated to ticket it.

It's a Gusher!

We're rich, I tells ya, rich! It's the **World's Largest Oil** Derrick. Excavating crude oil in Redwater, Alberta, this big rig stands 51 metres tall.

High Sticking

You are certain to get a high-sticking penalty if you bring the **World's Tallest and Heaviest Hockey Stick** onto the ice. Measuring 63 metres in height and weighing an impressive 2.8 tonnes, the stick was crafted out of a Douglas-fir tree and reinforced with steel. Currently located in Duncan, British Columbia, the oversized stick was built for Vancouver's Expo '86. It was awarded to the city of Duncan in a Canada-wide contest held following the fair.

Swing It!

Shuttlecock! It's the **World's Largest Badminton Racquet**. Swinging in St. Albert, Alberta, this piece of sports equipment stands 4.3 metres tall and weighs 225 kilograms.

Real Fun-guys

Mushaboom! It's the **World's Largest Mushrooms**. Growing in Vilna, Alberta, the "Mushroom Capital of Alberta," these furious fungi stand six metres tall, while the mushroom caps measure between three and 4.6 metres across.

Canadian Curiosities

In May 2003, Nick Calderaro of Scarborough, Ontario, concocted the **World's Largest Jawbreaker**, which weighed nearly 13 kilograms.

Egg-gad!

Oy-yoy! It's the **World's Largest Pysanka**. Hatched in Vegreville, Alberta, this enormous Ukrainian Easter egg is 9.4 metres tall, 5.5 metres wide and weighs 2270 kilograms. This engineering marvel features 524 star patterns, 1108 equilateral triangles, 3512 visible facets, 6978 nuts and bolts and 177 internal struts. Over 3500 pieces of aluminum were used in its construction.

T-Rex Trouble

Ruling Drumheller, Alberta, the **World's Largest Dinosaur**, a terrifying *Tyrannosaurus rex*, stands 25 metres tall, is 46 metres long and weighs 66 tonnes. Adventurous visitors can climb up 106 steps inside the dino to an observation platform in its mouth.

Too Good to Eat

Pass the sour cream! It's the **World's Largest Perogy**, complete with giant fork. Fried up in Glendon, Alberta, this towering tasty treat stands 6.2 metres tall and weighs 2700 kilograms.

This Boot Was Made for Walkin'

Kicking it in Edmonton, Alberta, the **World's Largest Western Boot** stands 12 metres tall and is an advertisement for the Stallion Boot and Jean Company.

A Cool Place to Live

Come on into the **World's Largest Dome Igloo**. Measuring 7.85 metres tall, the igloo has an interior diameter of 7.85 metres and an internal height of 4.17 metres. Spearheaded by the Association of Professional Engineers and Geoscientists of New Brunswick, the ice-cold condo was completed in Grand Falls, New Brunswick, on February 17, 2008, with the help of 72 volunteers.

Holy Smoke!

While smoking a pipe is bad thing, building the **World's Biggest Smoking Pipe** is great thing. Measuring six metres long, 1.5 metres in height and weighing 195 kilograms, this piece of smoking paraphernalia can be seen fuming in St. Claude, Manitoba.

A Grave Matter

Located in L'Anse Amour, Newfoundland and Labrador, **North America's Oldest Burial Mound** is over 7500 years old and marks the gravesite of an adolescent boy. The circular mound is eight metres in diameter and is covered with large boulders.

Spud-tacular

Hungry? It's the **World's Largest Exhibit of Potato Artifacts**. Located in O'Leary, Prince Edward Island, the PEI Potato Museum features an array of farm equipment and machinery that was used to grow and harvest potatoes. You'll also want to keep an "eye" out for the museum's top spud, a 4.2-metre-high potato that guards the museum's front entrance.

Quazy Quizzes

1. How far was the world's longest ramp jump on a snowmobile?
    A. 66.14 metres
    B. 77.05 metres
    C. 80.31 metres
    D. The snowmobile never landed.

2. What is the most common lake name in Canada?
    A. Long Lake
    B. Moose Lake
    C. Mud Lake
    D. Rake Lake

3. What is the most common place name in Canada?
    A. Mount Pleasant
    B. Springfield
    C. Richmond
    D. Happyville

Answers on page 242.

Monumental Match Up

A passing radioactive comet has brought the "Giants of the Prairies" to life. Needless to say, when they came began animated, many of the massive monuments decided to move around the country. Now, as an employee of the Canadian Tourism Commission, it is your job to round up the colossal constructions and return them to their prairie homes.

Barrhead, Alberta	World's First UFO Landing Pad
Beaverlodge, Alberta	World's Largest Ukrainian Sausage
Edmonton, Alberta	World's Largest Bunnock
Vegreville, Alberta	World's Largest Dinosaur
Vulcan, Alberta	Canada's Largest Baseball Bat
Komarno, Manitoba	Giant Pysanka (Easter Egg)
Macklin, Saskatchewan	Giant Star Trek
St. Paul, Alberta	The Happy Rock
Drumheller, Alberta	World's Largest Mosquito
Torrington, Alberta	World's Largest Beaver
Gladstone, Manitoba	Giant Gopher
Mundare, Alberta	World's Largest Blue Heron

Answers on page 243.

Jumbo Jumble

A life-size mastodon replica has come to life and is running amok in downtown Stewiacke, Nova Scotia. Unfortunately, all the synonyms that the local media outlets were planning to use to describe the monster's size have been mixed up. Now, as the local news teleprompter, it is your job to unravel the descriptors before the six o'clock news.

AEMLP _____

BZSELIA _____

NSTLSBATUAI _____

NMIESEM _____

OMRNSOEU _____

UOSOPDIIRG _____

EDSNUTROEM _____

OUSNTDSPEU _____

ANNRATUGGA _____

ELTPAIHNNEE _____

ITMAONNSUOU _____

EOIRGNWT _____

OSMOUVUINL _____

WGINHOPP _____

OHUGNSUOM _____

IAACNOSRMOTL _____

OGUROMINS _____

ULBYK _____

UEAIBMSAMLRE _____

GIGNCTAI _____

Answers on page 243.

The _____est Marvels

Giant Crossword

The government of Canada wants to build a massive monument of you made entirely out of margarine. However, before they order in loads of the creamy, yellow goodness, you must first prove that you are butter than everyone else by completing this crossword.

ACROSS

1. A tree chopper in Goodsoil, Saskatchewan
5. A Ukrainian dumpling in Glendon, Alberta
7. A winter friend in Beardmore, Ontario
9. A tall tuber in Maugerville, New Brunswick
10. A pest in Wabamun, Alberta
11. An early riser in Shediac, New Brunswick
13. A towering tuned instrument in Sydney, Cape Breton
14. A mined mineral in Sudbury, Ontario

DOWN

2. A woolly one in Kyle, Saskatchewan
3. A whooping one in Govan, Saskatchewan
4. An authorization in Humboldt, Saskatchewan
6. A pest in Ogema, Saskatchewan
7. A Christmas character in Watson, Saskatchewan
8. A harrowing hatchet in Nackawic, New Brunswick
12. A reel tall one in Houston, British Columbia
15. A mammoth milker in Sussex, New Brunswick

Answers on page 243.

Comment Collecting

Tourists say the darnedest things when they see one of Canada's many giant marvels. Unfortunately, there are so many people talking at once it is hard to make out what praise they have to bestow upon our world-record-setting statues, landmarks and monuments. As an employee of Tourism Canada, it is your job to sort through the conversations and locate the good comments and exclamations to post on our website.

```
S G A D Z O O K S R A I L U C E P E C R E
P F A R F E T C H E D Y E N U S E L U E Q
E L L A B D D O U R Y N S D B T A D R M Z
C A A M A Z I N G E N N G E E U L O I A M
T M G E D P E Z E E N A R R S Q L U O R N
A R A N R E W O W U A C S U R C E T U K G
C O D L U C O E A Q N N N E I B S S S A N
L N Z I S U G E I U E U E C T R T T E B I
E B O P B N D R V R C I T S A T N A F L Y
P A E S A E D I E A D E A Q U U E N L E F
U O S R E S O E C C E N T R I C D D L L I
Z O T U Z W B O E V I S S E R P M I A R T
Z S U N B E L I E V A B L E S A A N B C S
L E E S A B U I N C R E D I B L E G S E Y
I P R A L U C A T C E P S P A E S E E A M
N C A M B A F F L I N G O E E R R A Z I B
G A W E S O M E A E A S T C O R A Z Z I B
```

Strange	Unusual	Incredible	Spectacular	Puzzling
Weird	Abnormal	Absurd	Spectacle	Baffling
Oddball	Wow	Farfetched	Peculiar	Bizzaro
Uncanny	Amazing	Unbelievable	Curious	Mystifying
Eerie	Outstanding	Fantastic	Queer	Awesome
Eccentric	Impressive	Remarkable	Bizarre	Gadzooks

Answers to Quizzes and Puzzles

The _____est Canadian: Games People Play

Answers to Quiz

1. D.   At the conclusion of the CBC's Greatest Canadian Challenge, Tommy Douglas, politician and father of medicare, was announced as the winner.

2. B.   Saguenay, Québec, has the lowest crime rate in the country.

3. C.   More Canadians die in motorized vehicle accidents than by poisoning, electrocution or suffocation.

4. B.   At the age of 39, Joseph Clark was the youngest Canadian prime minster.

5. C.   Donald Winfield passed 5704 kidney stones naturally.

6. B.   Richmond, BC, residents have an average life expectancy of 81.2 years.

7. A.   Fracture

8. D.   In fact, Guinness received 16 claims for the "World's longest nipple hair," "Most pickle juice drank" and "Most times pride swallowed." Surprisingly, none of the aforementioned records made it into the record book.

9. B.   With a life expectancy of only 65.4 years, folks in Nunavut are far below the Canadian average life expectancy, which is around 80.6 years.

Answers to Timelines

Get a driver's licence = Denarian (10 to 19 years)

Graduate from university = Vicenarian (20 to 29 years)

Retire = Sexagenarian (60 to 69 years)

Get married = Tricenarian (30 to 39 years)

Enter the *Guinness Book of Records* = Supercentenarian (110+ years)

Celebrate your last Christmas, maybe = Nonagenarian (90 to 99 years)

Have a midlife crisis = Quadragenarian (40 to 49 years)

Have your birthday announced on the *Today* show = Centenarian (100 to 109 years)

Spoil your grandchildren = Septuagenarian (70 to 79 years)

Move to a care home = Octogenarian (80 to 89 years)

Be eligible for the seniors' menu = Quinquagenarian (50 to 59 years)

Answers to Immigration Frustration

Afghanistan; Antarctica; Argentina; Australia; Bangladesh; Croatia; Ethiopia; Guadeloupe; Indonesia; Jamaica; Zimbabwe; Venezuela; Uruguay; Swaziland; Somalia; Philippines; Nicaragua; Laos; Madagascar; America

Answers to Career Crossroads

ACROSS: 4. Electrician   12. Daredevil
         5. Musician   13. Firefighter
         8. Politician   14. Accountant
         9. Ballerina   16. Architect
        10. Bartender

DOWN: 1. Geologist   8. Painter
         2. Banker   11. Writer
         3. Pilot   12. Doctor
         6. Plumber   15. Baker
         7. Lawyer

The _____est Climate: Quizzard Warning

Answers to Quiz

1. B. At an elevation of 1089 metres above sea level, Airdrie, Alberta, is the highest Canadian city.

2. A. At an elevation of 1540 metres above sea level, Lake Louise is the highest.

3. C. On February 3, 1937, in Snag, Yukon, the mercury dipped to a record-setting −63°C.

4. B. On July 5, 1937, in Midale, Saskatchewan, the mercury rose to an unprecedented 45°C.

5. A. Located in south-central British Columbia, Kamloops experienced 24 straight days of temperatures over 35°C in 1958.

6. C. With an annual rainfall of 427.81 millimetres, Saskatchewan is the driest province in Canada. However, the territory of Nunavut receives less annual rainfall than that.

7. B. With an annual snowfall of 443.13 centimetres, Gander, Newfoundland and Labrador, is packed with flakes—snowflakes, that is.

8. C. In 1978, Whitesand, Saskatchewan, endured 180 days of rain.

9. C. On February 11, 1999, Tahtsa Lake West, British Columbia, received 145 centimetres of snow in the span of 24 hours.

10. A. With an annual average wind speed of 19.7 kilometres per hour, Swift Current is the windiest Saskatchewan city.

Answers to Inclement Weather Connector

Regina = Cyclone; Winnipeg = Flooding; Québec = Ice storm; Newfoundland = Tsunami; Edmonton = Tornado; British Columbia = Avalanche; Maritimes = Nor'easter; Northwest Territories = Wind chill; Ontario = Thunderstorm

Answers to Torrential Textual Twisters

Almanac; Meteorologist; Visibility; Thermometer; Breeze; Condensation; Drought; Evaporation; Lightning; Precipitation; Humidity; Jet stream; Anemometer; Cloud; Environment; Drifting; Cumulus; Clear; Clipper; Advisory

Answers to Crossword Play

ACROSS:
2. Rainbow
5. Whiteout
8. Blizzard
9. Summer

11. Tsunami
13. Showers
15. Blanket
16. Umbrella

DOWN:
1. Freeze
3. Wind
4. Floods
6. Erosion

7. Sunrise
10. Fog
12. Shovel
14. Radar

The _____est Beasts: Animal Testing

Answers to Quiz

1. B. Persian
2. C. Labrador
3. A. Trout

Answers to Animal Rescue

Nova Scotia = Bobcat; Saskatchewan = Pronghorn; Manitoba = Polar bear; British Columbia = Orca; Alberta = Mountain goat; Ontario = Flying squirrel; Québec = Wild boar; Newfoundland = Red fox; Prince Edward Island = Lobster; New Brunswick = Puffin; Yukon = Moose; Northwest Territories = Beluga; Nunavut = Caribou

Answers to Bewildered Beasts

Weasel; Seal; Caribou; Marmot; Bobcat; Coyote; Skunk; Vole; Wolverine; Snake; Walrus; Bison; Elk; Chipmunk; Woodchuck; Cougar; Whale; Muskox; Antelope

Answers to Animal Crossing

ACROSS:
1. Dinosaur
3. Mammal
4. Hibernation
7. Reptile

9. Nocturnal
10. Cobweb
11. Vertebrate
13. Omnivore

DOWN:
2. Spider
3. Monkey
4. Hamster
5. Nest

6. Sheep
8. Horse
10. Cage
12. Teeth

The _____est Landscape: Land Minds

Answers to Quiz

1. A. British Columbia has only 861 lakes over three square kilometres in size.

2. C. With an area of 44,807 square kilometres, Wood Buffalo National Park, which is located on the border of Alberta and the Northwest Territories, is bigger than all of Switzerland.

3. B. With a current of 16 knots (or three kilometres per hour) or more, the Nakwakto Rapids in Slingsby Channel, British Columbia, are the strongest.

4. B. Located in the Northwest Territories, the Mackenzie River stretches 1738 kilometres.

5. C. With a shoreline that stretches 12,268 kilometres, Hudson Bay covers an area of 1,233,000 square kilometres.

Answers to Continental Drifting

Alberta = Badlands; Prince Edward Island = Red Soil; Newfoundland and Labrador = Churchill River; New Brunswick = Bay of Fundy; Nova Scotia = Sable Island; Ontario = Niagara Falls; Québec = Saint Lawrence River; Manitoba = Red River; Saskatchewan = Cypress Hills; British Columbia = Giant Douglas-firs; Yukon = Mount Logan; Northwest Territories = Great Slave Lake; Nunavut = Rankin Inlet

Answers to Landmass Destruction

Mountain; Valley; Elevation; Longitude; Latitude; Degrees; River; Lake; Whirlpool; Range; Field; Creek; Bay; Aquifer; Archipelago; Atoll; Geography; Axis; Brook; Rock

Answers to Across Canada

ACROSS:
1. Continent
2. Hemisphere
4. Floodplain
6. Bedrock
7. Island
9. Glacier
11. Desert
13. Fauna
15. Estuary

DOWN:
1. Cove
2. Heartland
3. Shrub
4. Fault
5. Earth
8. Delta
10. Map
12. Tree
14. Gulf

The _____est Athletes: Mental Workout

Answers to Quiz

1. B. Steve Yzerman from Cranbrook, British Columbia, was captain of the Detroit Red Wings for 20 years, from 1986 to 2006.

2. C. In his 26-season NHL career, Gordie Howe played 1767 games.

3. A. With a final score of 14–7, the number of goals scored in the Montréal Canadiens vs. Toronto St. Patricks game on January 10, 1920, totalled 21—still the most goals scored between two teams in a single game.

4. B. One of the "Original Six" NHL teams, the Montréal Canadiens won their first Stanley Cup in 1916, a year before the NHL was even founded. After the NHL was formed, they went on to win 23 more times.

Answers to The Line of Scrubbage

Hockey = Neck guard; Badminton = Shuttlecock; Football = Neck roll; Soccer = Shin guards; Lacrosse = Crosse; Baseball = Base; Tennis = Sweatbands; Skiing = Goggles; Golf = Tee; Archery = Finger tab; Auto racing = Seat belt; Bowling = Pin; Gymnastics = Leotard; Kayaking = Spray skirt; Running = Spikes

Answers to Word Game Misconduct

Homerun; Bunt; Walk; Strike; Boots; Alpine; Blitz; Block; Backfield; Slashing; Offside; Offence; Officials; Arena; Assist; Linesman; Period; Player; Point; Catcher

Answers to Lacrosse Word

ACROSS:
3. Eskimos
6. Overtime
7. Zamboni
10. Interception
12. Tripping
13. Foul
14. Freestyle
16. Strike
18. Bombers

DOWN:
1. Puck
2. Save
4. Stealing
5. Whistle
8. Zone
9. Astroturf
11. Carve
15. Lions
17. Eagle

The _____est Construction: Skill Building

Answers to Quiz

1. C. In 1999, the *Rocky Mountaineer* passenger train travelled from Vancouver, British Columbia, to Banff, Alberta, with a total of 41 passenger cars.

2. B. Although its main focus is the 1988 Winter Olympics, the gold medal for the world's largest Olympic museum goes to Calgary.

3. B. Sydney, Nova Scotia, is the home address of Canada's oldest continuously operating post office, established in 1784.

4. D. Built in 1759, the lighthouse located on Sambro Island, Nova Scotia, is still flashing sailors over 250 years after it was constructed.

5. B. Lying in both Alberta and the Northwest Territories, Wood Buffalo National Park is the largest national park in Canada, with 44,807 square kilometres.

6. C. With a total enrollment of 74,760, the University of Toronto is the big man on campus.

7. D. With nearly 25 people per square kilometre, Prince Edward Island really packs 'em in.

8. B. Toronto, where you're one in 2.5 million.

9. A. Established in 1670 as a trading post, the Hudson's Bay Company is one of the oldest commercial corporations in the entire world.

10. C. Located 440 metres above sea level, Prince Albert is as low as cities go in Saskatchewan.

Answers to Skyscraper Scavenger Hunt

Yellowknife = Centre Square

Halifax = Fenwick Place

St. John's = John Cabot Building

Winnipeg = Canwest Place

Regina = Delta Regina Hotel

Toronto = First Canadian Place

Calgary = Suncor Energy Centre West

Montréal = 1250 René-Lévesque

Vancouver = Living Shangri-La

Edmonton = Manulife Place

Charlottetown = Delta Prince Edward

Saskatoon = La Renaissance Apartments

Moncton = Assumption Place

Whitehorse = Yukon Legislative Building

Nunavut = Legislative Building of Nunavut

Answers to Word Shambles

Studs; Grout; Mortar; Joint; Vertical; Brick; Fastened; Frame; Tile; Wall; Attic; Ventilators; Highway; Dam; Bridge; Skyscraper; Subway; Clipper; Church; Barn

Answers to Building Acrossword

ACROSS:
2. Foundation
3. Tension
7. Insulation
8. Walkway
10. Suspension
12. Tower
15. Stadium
16. Basement
17. Unstable

DOWN:
1. Ledge
4. Iron
5. Nail
6. Truss
8. Window
9. Wood
11. Dome
13. Pipes
14. Cable

The _____est Marvels: Quazy Quizzes

Answers to Quiz

1. C. In 2007, Ross Mercer of Whitehorse, Yukon, jumped 80.31 metres on his snowmobile.
2. A. There are 203 lakes in Canada named Long Lake.
3. A. There are 16 areas in Canada with the name Mount Pleasant.

Answers to Monumental Match Up

Barrhead, Alberta = World's Largest Blue Heron

Beaverlodge, Alberta = World's Largest Beaver

Edmonton, Alberta = Canada's Largest Baseball Bat

Vegreville, Alberta = Giant Pysanka (Ukrainian Easter Egg)

Vulcan, Alberta = Giant Star Trek *Enterprise*

Komarno, Manitoba = World's Largest Mosquito

Macklin, Saskatchewan = World's Largest Bunnock

St. Paul, Alberta = World's First UFO Landing Pad

Drumheller, Alberta = World's Largest Dinosaur

Torrington, Alberta = Giant Gopher

Gladstone, Manitoba = The Happy Rock

Mundare, Alberta = World's Largest Ukrainian Sausage

Answers to Jumbo Jumble

Ample; Sizable; Substantial; Immense; Enormous; Prodigious; Tremendous; Stupendous; Gargantuan; Elephantine; Mountainous; Towering; Voluminous; Whopping; Humongous; Astronomical; Ginormous; Bulky; Immeasurable; Gigantic

Answers to Giant Crossword

ACROSS:
1. Lumberjack
5. Perogy
7. Snowman
9. Potato
10. Dragonfly
11. Rooster
13. Fiddle
14. Nickel

DOWN:
2. Mammoth
3. Crane
4. Stamp
6. Grasshopper
7. Santa
8. Axe
12. Rod
15. Cow

Other Places to Find out About Record-Breaking Stuff

Web Sources

Big Things: The Monuments of Canada: www.bigthings.ca

The Canadian Encyclopedia: www.thecanadianencyclopedia.com

Canadian Geographic: www.canadiangeographic.ca

Canadian Olympic Committee: www.olympic.ca

Canadian Wildlife Federation: www.cwf-fcf.org

CBC Kids: www.cbc.ca/kids/

CN Tower: www.cntower.ca

Funology: www.funology.com

Guinness World Records: www.guinnessworldrecords.com

Hockey Canada: www.hockeycanada.ca

How Stuff Works: www.howstuffworks.com

Jay Cochrane: www.jaycochrane.com

The Joggler: www.thejoggler.ca

Large Canadian Roadside Attractions: www.roadsideattractions.ca

Mrs. Mitchell's Virtual School for Kids: www.kathimitchell.com/Canada/canada.htm

Proud Canadian Kids: www.proudcanadiankids.ca

Ripley's Believe It or Not!: www.ripley's.com

Top 10 of Everything: www.top10ofeverything.com

Travel for Kids: www.travelforkids.com

Virtual Museum of Canada: www.virtualmuseum.ca

Wikipedia: www.wikipedia.org

World Records Academy: www.worldrecordacademy.org

Yahoo! Kids: www.kids.yahoo.com

Zoom School: www.zoomschool.com/school/Canada/

Books

Ash, Russell. *Top 10 of Everything 2010*. New York: Sterling, 2009.

Biberstein, René. *Bathroom Book of Ontario Trivia*. Edmonton: Blue Bike, 2006.

Fleming, Andrew. *Bathroom Book of Atlantic Canada Trivia*. Edmonton: Blue Bike, 2007.

Fleming, Andrew. *Bathroom Book of British Columbia Trivia*. Edmonton: Blue Bike, 2006.

Gifford, Clive. *Atlas of Firsts: A World of Amazing Record Breakers*. London, UK: Kingfisher, 2009.

Guinness World Records 2010. London, UK: Guinness Media, 2009.

MacFarlane, Glenda. *Bathroom Book of Saskatchewan Trivia*. Edmonton: Blue Bike, 2007.

Michaelides, Marina. *Bathroom Book of Alberta Trivia*. Edmonton: Blue Bike, 2006.

Murphy, Angela. *Bathroom Book of Canadian Trivia*. Edmonton: Blue Bike, 2005.

Ripley's Believe It or Not! Special Edition 2010. New York: Scholastic, 2009.

Wojna, Lisa. *Bathroom Book of Manitoba Trivia*. Edmonton: Blue Bike, 2007.

About the Illustrators

Djordje Todorovic

Djordje Todorovic is an artist/illustrator living in Toronto, Ontario. He first moved to the city to go to York University to study fine arts. It was there that he got a taste for illustrating while working as the illustrator for his college paper, Mondo Magazine. He has since worked on various projects and continues to perfect his craft. Aside from his artistic work, Djordje devotes his time volunteering at the Print and Drawing Centre at the Art Gallery of Ontario. When he is not doing that, he is out trotting the globe.

Roger Garcia

Roger Garcia is a self-taught artist with some formal training who specializes in cartooning and illustration. He is an immigrant from El Salvador, and during the last few years, his work has been primarily cartoons and editorial illustrations in pen and ink. Recently, he has started painting once more, focusing on simplifying the human form, using a bright minimal palette and as few elements as possible. His work can be seen in newspapers, magazines and promo material and on www.rogergarcia.ca.

Peter Tyler

Peter is a recent graduate of the Vancouver Film School programs in visual art and design, and classical animation. Though his ultimate passion is filmmaking, he is also intent on developing his draftsmanship and storytelling, with the aim of using those skills in future filmic misadventures.

Patrick Hénaff

A native of France, Patrick Hénaff is mostly self-taught and is a versatile artist who has explored a variety of mediums under many different influences. He now uses primarily pen and ink to draw and then processes the images on computer. He is particularly interested in the narrative power of pictures and tries to use them as a way to tell stories, whether he is working on comic pages, posters, illustrations, cartoons or concept art.

Graham Johnson

Graham Johnson is an Edmonton-based illustrator and graphic designer. When he isn't drawing or designing, he...well...he's always drawing or designing! On the off-chance that you catch him not doing one of those things, he's probably cooking, playing tennis or poring over other illustrations.

About the Author

Shane Sellar

Shane Sellar lives in Calgary, Alberta. He is a former journalist who left the news trade to pursue other forms of writing, like poetry and books. He recently married his college sweetheart, and looks forward to many years of telling hilarious wife-related jokes. He holds no world or Canadian records, though he did write this biography during one of the worst blizzards of 2009. This is Shane's second book for Blue Bike—the first was *The Canadian Book of Birthdays*.